BLACK OPS PIZZA MARKETING

How the independent pizza restaurant can compete against the big chain stores and win

Paul Baker

Black Ops Pizza Marketing
How the Independent Pizza Restaurant Can
Compete Against the Big Chain Stores and Win

© 2015 Paul Baker

Table of Contents

Introduction To Black Ops Marketing.................................6

The Parthenon Principle.................................13

Marketing Incest.................................16

Image Advertising Vs. Direct Response Advertising.................................19

Your USP.................................25

Lifetime Value Of A Client.................................35

Herd Data Base.................................44

Raising Prices.................................48

Direct Mail Letters.................................58

A.I.D.A.................................68

Grabbers.................................86

Voice
Broadcasting...92

24 Hour Toll Free Recorded
Messages...98

Free Pizza
Letters...107

Lazy Customer
Letters...118

Multi Sequence/Mucked Up
Mailings...124

Endorsed
Mailings...138

Postcards..143

Testimonials...146

Texting..156

Thank You Bounce Back
Card...163

Using Disasters To Generate
Cash..167

Warning Labels On
Boxes..173

Your
Guarantee...176

Fundraising Letters……………………………………………...180

Everyone Wins contest………………………………………..187

Referrals………………………………………………..191

Getting In Front Of The Decision Makers……………………………………………....195

How To Create Newspaper Ads For Maximum Profits…………………………………198

How To Get Free Publicity……………………………215

The $500 Launch…………………………………………262

What To Do When A Competitor Shuts Down………………………………………………...267

255 Of The Greatest Headlines Ever Written………………………………………………272

Conclusion………………………………………………..290

Resources……………………………………………...293

<u>Introduction</u>

Do you have a marketing budget the size of Wal-Mart?

No? What about Pepsi or Coke? Not quite? Hmm….
What about Pizza Hut, Dominoes or Papa Johns, you're in
the same type of business as those three, surely you have a
marketing budget that's equal to those.

What's that? You don't have a marketing budget that's
several hundred thousand dollars every month like they do?

Then why the heck would you try to do the same marketing
that they do? As an independent operator or someone with
only a few stores, you can't go head to head with the big
boys and play their game.

Let's look at it this way. Pretend you own your own small
island. Its only say about 50 miles long, and 50 miles wide.

Not only do you own this small island, but you're also the
leader of this island. Your people love and respect you,
everything is good on your island.

Then one day, a large military force from a neighboring
island arrives on your beach. This military force has
10,000 men, 1000 tanks, and 100 fighter jets.

Unfortunately for you, they have only one goal. To
eliminate you, and take your islands resources.

Luckily, you have your own military of 500 men, so you lead your army onto the field. As you approach the opposing army, you see that they're already lined up for battle and ready to charge.

Suddenly the enemy commander gives the order, and the enemy army surges forward at your small army. Well you think to yourself, if they're charging at us, it's obviously the best tactic, so I'm going to charge too!

With that final thought, you give your men the order to charge the enemy!

Pretty stupid huh. Not only would you be completely annihilated, but the opposing army would probably get a good laugh out of your assault.

However, this is how most pizza store owners run their business. The big franchise does a $10 pizza deal... so you do a $10 pizza deal, or if you get really aggressive, you do a $9.99 deal.

If the big chain store does mass advo mailings with lots of coupons, then you send out your own advo fliers.

See the similarities? Even though the coupons might vary some, you're still using marketing tactics that the big boys use on a daily basis.

Now let's look at our island scenario in a different way.

The enemy general lines up his forces ready to charge, however, there's one problem. Your army is nowhere to be seen.

Thinking you probably gave up and ran away from his much larger force, he commands his first battalion to take the equipment to the other side of the island and begin gathering its resources.

His first lieutenant tells him that unfortunately last night there was an explosion and all the equipment was destroyed.

The next morning the general tells his first lieutenant to have his second battalion scout the east side of the island.

His first lieutenant tells him that unfortunately the second battalion apparently had their food rations go bad and most are dead or sick from poisoning, but the third battalion is ready to go in the second battalions place.

However… the third battalion might not have the leadership needed for the mission since the battalions leading captain accidentally fell on a knife last night and bled to death.

Furious, the general orders air strikes on your small island. But when the pilots inspect their jets, most of them have had their tires shot out so they can't even get to the runway.

The general calls his command center back at his island and tells them he needs more aircraft tires, ammunition and troops.

Unfortunately for him, the request for more materials and men has to go through all the proper channels and be signed off on by the appropriate people before the tires and equipment can be approved. They tell him that everything should be approved within a few months.

So the general waits, but during this time, more of his troops disappear. More of the food and water supplies go bad or end up missing, until eventually he says "You know... this island really isn't such a great island after all.

My intelligence showed me that this island was rich in resources and was easy pickings, but that's not the case at all. We should probably just call it quits and cut our losses."

And with that, the opposing army loads up and finds another small island to conquer. One that doesn't know not to engage them head on.

Now this may seem like a goofy analogy, but if you ran your marketing by using black ops tactics, striking only targets you knew you could hit and be successful at, wouldn't that be a better strategy than trying to match a superior force or business?

What I'm going to show you in this book is how you can use these black ops tactics to cripple, and eventually eliminate your competition. These tactics are proven marketing tactics, not just theories, and they will quickly increase your pizza sales if implemented.

The big corporate stores can't compete with these strategies and tactics. They don't have the speed, and in some cases the desire to implement them. I know this for a fact. I was on a marketing and brand development board for a major pizza franchise for 18 months.

I actually recommended some of these strategies and showed them how they could use them to increase their profits. Their response... "That's too difficult to implement" or "that might work for one store, but it wont work for 200" or "That's too expensive."

The last excuse was pretty much the last straw for me. Ya, some of these tactics will cost more to implement than just running an advo coupon dump, <u>but if they make you money every time you use them, why would you not use it</u>?

 It's like someone sitting at a slot machine. You put in $100 and the machine spits out $200. If you knew this slot machine was going to do this every time, would you not sit there and keep feeding in $100 dollar bills until the machine stopped spitting out the $200?

Or would you say "Gee… I know this machine is going to give me $200 if I play it, but gosh… $100 is a lot of money to put in it, I think I'll keep my $100."

I resigned from that position and let them continue their ineffective advertising techniques, which usually consisted of doing a banner and box toppers every three months.

Nothing wrong with using banners and box toppers (box toppers can be extremely effective) but when that's your core marketing, you're in trouble. At the time of this writing, I seen they only had 187 stores where they had 222 a few years earlier.

They may still be able to turn things around, but only if they implement new marketing strategies and tactics that will bring in greater sales and results.

Now before we get into brass tactics, I need to warn you. These marketing strategies are not the usual strategies that you're used to seeing.

Ya, there's some box topper and postcard strategies, but most of these will be unconventional and something that you've never seen used in the pizza industry before.

These are tactics that will quickly double your sales and income. That's what their designed to do, generate cash. They are not designed to get your logo or name in front of people.

They are not designed to make you feel good about your business or to generate name recognition. Only to generate sales and cash.

Here's one of the best examples I can think of to show you what I mean.

Remember the Taco Bell chihuahua? Ya, who doesn't.

When the executives at Taco Bell did a recall test to see how many people remembered the ads with the Chihuahua in it, they had almost 100% of the people that they questioned remember the ad.

For these big companies, that's what they consider a successful advertising campaign.

Because everyone remembered these commercials, the Taco Bell big wigs, the advertising agency, and the marketing director at Taco Bell decided to keep running these ads for another couple of years.

There was just one problem. Sales at Taco Bell started dropping when they started running these ads, and continued to drop, and drop and drop for year after year, as long as they kept running these doggie ads.

So they had an ad that practically everyone on the planet could remember, but it didn't generate sales. The Taco Bell franchisees were up in arms about this. Their livelihoods depended on them being able to sell tacos.

Eventually, because of the drop in sales, and the reluctance to stop running the chihuahua ads, the advertising agency, marketing director, and the president of Taco Bell were all fired by the board, and the company went back to actually advertising their food.

Here's the point. The purpose of marketing is not so people remember your ad. It's to bring in cold hard cash to your business.

With this book you're going to learn very quickly that if an ad doesn't generate money, you're going to get rid of it - no matter how cute or memorable the ad is. An ads only purpose is to generate you cash.

The Parthenon Principle

One of the foundations of this course is the Parthenon business model of marketing your pizzeria. This principle is what I believe to be the strongest and safest way to operate your business.

The alternative to the Parthenon principle is the diving board model of business. This is how most pizza restaurants unknowingly operate their businesses.

If you look at how a diving board is made, it has one single base, then a board that's attached to that base. The board is your sales, and that one single base that is supporting the board is the one type of advertising or revenue generating activity that you and most other restaurants use.

This could be anything from newspaper ads or fliers to having a high traffic location. But whatever it is, it's the one pillar of your sales.

Now what happens when that one pillar or base that is generating 70%, 80%, 90%, or even 100% of your revenue is broken or taken away?

What if all of a sudden, that great high traffic location that has generated all your revenue is taken away because of a road widening project that will take 1-2 years to complete and all that traffic is being diverted around your restaurant?

What if that newspaper that you've been advertising in for years that brings in lots of customers suddenly goes bankrupt and shuts down?

What if that awesome manager with the magnetic personality suddenly decides to leave you and go open their own restaurant?

The point is, anytime you depend solely on that one pillar to bring in and sustain the revenue and sales for your business, and then that pillar is removed – you're screwed.

The alternative to the diving board model is the Parthenon model.

The Parthenon is this huge concrete building in Greece that is supported by a large number of massive and strong pillars.

It has survived thousands of years of the elements beating down upon it. It has survived hundreds of wars. It has even survived when a military unit used it as a munitions storage and some of the munitions went off, destroying and damaging some of the pillars.

And yet it still stands strong, and will remain so long after you and I are gone.

Now imagine building your restaurant using the Parthenon model where you have 6, 8, 10, or 20 pillars supporting your business, and each of those pillars representing a process, activity, system that brings in revenue.

Now what happens if one of those pillars are removed? Your restaurant is still strong and is still standing.

Sure, there might be some damage, from the one pillar being removed suddenly, but you're not going to go bankrupt because of that one pillar.

Each time you implement and maintain one of the tactics in this course, you're adding another pillar to your restaurant.

I'm not suggesting that you overwhelm yourself and try to implement everything at once, however I do suggest that you take one or two tactics, and start implementing them into your restaurant.

When they become pillars and you can rely on them to generate sales and revenue, add another couple of strategies. Keep doing this until your pizzeria has enough income producing pillars to sustain itself if one or two of your sales producing pillars were to be suddenly removed.

__Are You Committing Incest?__

When you got started in your pizza store, where did you get most of your marketing ideas from? Most likely it was from some kind of pizza magazine, which is owned and written by people in the pizza industry.

Or maybe you were a member of some pizza trade association, which is run and organized by people in the pizza industry.

Or maybe it was from a franchisor that's in the pizza business, or maybe you got your ideas from a seminar or conference that's exclusive to the pizza industry.

Wherever you look, pizza store owners are looking inside their own industry for new marketing ideas and strategies.

This is called marketing incest, and just like real incest, over time everyone keeps getting dumber and dumber.

The real estate industry is one of the worst about doing this. Here's what usually happens. Little Susie goes to the real estate night classes (which is taught by someone in the real estate industry) and gets her license to sell homes.

A few days later, she gets her first listing. She's all excited and ready to start advertising her clients home, so she looks at the local newspaper, which is filled with hundreds of real estate listings.

She notices that <u>everyone</u> puts a picture of the house that their selling, and then a lot of abbreviated words like 2br, 1ba, ac, etc....

Well... If everyone else is doing their advertising like this, then it must work she thinks.

And she proceeds to place ads of the home she's listing in the paper just like everyone else. She then notices that <u>everyone</u> else puts a sign in the front yard.

Well... If everyone else is doing it, it must be working or they wouldn't be doing that. So Susie puts a sign in the front yard.

A few weeks later, Susie goes to her first real estate seminar, which is taught by... you guessed it, other real estate brokers in her industry. They tell her that everyone is handing out business cards with their pictures on them.

Well... If everyone else is handing out business cards with their pictures on them, then it must work.

So Susie pays for a bunch of business cards with her picture on them that says something like "I have the keys to your new home" and her phone number.

See where this is going? Ya, Susie might get lucky and sell the house and get her commission, but were any of the ideas she received inside her own industry break through ideas?

The same thing happens in the pizza industry. Everyone is using box toppers, so it must work. Or the idea that since all the big chains are using advo for advertising, then it must be working.

The idea here is that you need to look outside your own industry for new ideas and opportunities. Look through other trade magazines and journals outside the pizza industry.

Talk to other business owners and see what they're doing in their marketing, then try to see if you can adapt it to the pizza industry.

Hair club for men used a marketing technique from the cell phone industry to launch its business from just a few offices to over 60 offices, and became the number one hair replacement firm in the world.

They noticed that most cell phone stores would give away the cell phone if you signed up for a one or two year contract. People were thrilled to get the phone free. So Hair Club For Men started giving away hair for free!

They would give you the free hair, and in return, you agreed to sign a yearly contract that you would be in once a month for a wash, cut, and whatever else they did to maintain the hair.

This one tactic launched them from being just another hair replacement company to the number one hair replacement company in the world.

Image Advertising – You don't Look As Good As You Think You Do

There's only two kinds of advertising that you can do. The first is image advertising. This is where a company basically puts its name out there, trying to display some kind of image.

Most of the corporate world uses this type of advertising, and it's what most colleges teach to their advertising students.

Basically when a company uses image advertising, they're telling everyone how great or friendly they are, or how much better they are than their competition.

Would you try to convince someone to buy your pizza by showing them a copy of your logo, or telling them how long you've been in business?

This type of advertising might (and I do stress might) be a viable form of advertising for an extremely large company like Coca Cola.

But when a small business does this type of advertising, its suicide.

Unfortunately, this is the kind of advertising that over 95% of pizza store owners use. They put out fliers with their name and logo on them.

Or the managers or owners will hand out business cards with the stores logo and their names on them.

Seriously… think back to the last time you actually bought anything because someone gave you their business card.

Better yet… when was the last time a customer came in saying "I just got this business card from the manager and I want to order a pizza"!

Go grab a copy of your local yellow pages and look through it. There's tons of examples of image advertising.

Logo, name, phone number, logo name phone number, that's what most of the yellow pages has in it.

If you're trying to use image advertising against a major pizza chain, who already has name recognition, you're going to spend yourself into bankruptcy.

I'm going to be very blunt here – <u>Dont do image advertising</u>!

The second type of advertising that you can use is called direct response advertising. This is the advertising that you're going to be learning to use in this course. Direct response is designed to "get a response" from the ad.

Direct response advertising uses a strong call to action, and uses human psychology to get customers to respond to the ad.

Let me be very clear, direct response advertising is not about using deep discounts to get people to respond. While there may be discounts or sales at times, there will always be a reason for the price discount.

There are also rules that we will follow when using direct response advertising.

1. **Never run an advertisement twice if it didn't work the first time.**

2. **Only run advertisements that you can track the results**

3. **Never fall in love with one of your ads**

Never run an advertisement twice if it didn't work the first time. I've seen people run the same ad or promotion over and over again because they believe the myth that someone needs to see an ad several times before it will begin to work on them.

This is probably one of the most financially catastrophic things you could do with your advertising.

If you spent $2000 on an advertisement, and that advertisement brought you in $100 in sales, why would you run the ad several more times?

That's insanity! According to Albert Einstein, the definition of insanity is doing the same thing over and over and expecting a different result.

If an ad doesn't bring you in a profit or at least break even, **stop running it**.

If you're breaking even on your ad, or even just taking a slight loss on it, and think you might be able to change a few things and make it profitable, go ahead and change some things and run it again.

Just don't keep running an ad that's not paying for itself very quickly.

Only run advertisements that you can track the results. This is another rule that you will want to follow to keep you out of the financial pitfalls.

If you can't track your ads, how will you know how many people are using them? How will you know if they're making you money, or losing you money?

You can't.

We've probably all had the guy that sells the back of grocery store receipts come in and try to sell us on this great idea (sarcasm there). You know which one I'm talking about don't you?

The one where you pay him several hundred bucks and he will get your name and a coupon on the back of the grocery store customers store receipt.

First, let me say that I've never heard of anyone making their money back on this.

Secondly, while you could tell if you made or lost money on this promotion by using a specific offer or coupon made specifically for this ad, there's no way to tell how many people received your coupon.

Did you show a profit off of 100 people or 10,000 people? Did you take a loss from 50 or 50,000?

Without the specific numbers, you can't track the results, and this is absolutely critical to any advertising campaign.

<u>Never fall in love with one of your ads</u>. This one is sometimes honestly hard to do. You'll spend days or weeks writing or laying out an ad. It's beautiful, it looks awesome, it's your work of art. You just know for sure its going to be a huge success.

You run the ad… and it flops.

You know for certain it flopped because you tested it. Out of 10,000 of these sent out, only 2 people responded to the offer, making you a return $19.00 on a $2800 investment.

Now most people, because they have fallen in love with the ad they created will for some reason run the ad again. After all, who couldn't possibly love this ad? It has a picture of my daughter in it.

And because they love their ad so much, they'll pay another $2800 to run the ad again, and take another $2,781 loss.

Remember what the definition of insanity was?

I know how it feels to spend days, sometimes weeks writing an ad, or working on a project. By the time you're done, you have so much time and sweat into it, you think it must work, but it doesn't.

If it fails, go ahead and cry over it. Set a timer for five minutes, then cry, scream, get mad, kick the dog, whatever you need to do to get it out of your system.

After five minutes, dry your eyes, put it behind you, and start on the next ad that needs to be worked on.

Don't dwell on it, and don't give up.

<u>Your USP</u>

This is gonna step on some toes, but here it goes... If you can't quickly articulate to someone why they should visit your pizzeria instead of your competitors... <u>You shouldn't be in business</u>!

Your USP <u>"Unique Selling Proposition"</u> is your way of concisely summing up why I should buy from you and nobody else.

And here's a hint... It can't be "Because we're the best" or "We're the friendliest restaurant in town" or "We're number one". These are pretty much what every other business uses, and it falls on deaf ears.

Here's an example of why you can't use the "We're number one" or "We're the best" for your USP.

I was watching a college football game one day a last year and it was a very lopsided game. The winning team was in the lead by a score of 31 to 0. At close to the end of the 4th quarter, the losing team got lucky, and I stress lucky, and managed to score a touchdown.

When their running back ran into the end zone and scored, what's the first thing he did?

He runs up to the camera, gives the "number 1" sign with his index finger and yells into the camera "Were number one baby"!

Um... ya... right.

This team was at the bottom in the ratings. They weren't even gonna win this game, much less be number one at anything in the near future.

So you see. When you stand there screaming how you're number one, or you're the best, it just comes off as puffery. It's just you beating your chest trying to make yourself look good, and nobody buys it.

Think back to the last time you bought anything because a company used the "We're the best" slogan. You might have bought something because someone else told you this company was the best, but that's completely different than someone saying it about themselves.

Your USP <u>must</u> separate you from the rest of the crowd. It has to be short, concise, and to the point.

I would be willing to bet that most business owners... yes I said owners, cant give you a good reason to buy from them instead of their competitors.

Your USP must tell people why to come to you instead of someone else. Here's two great examples of USPs that are concise and to the point.

When it absolutely, positively has to be there overnight

Hot fresh pizza delivered in 30 minutes or it's free

The first example is Federal Express's USP. It tells you exactly what they do, and why you should use them instead of someone else. If you were a business that had important documents that you needed to get across the country by the next day, would that get your attention?

The second example is from Domino's Pizza. And this USP literally created a pizza empire. It tells in one sentence why someone should order from them instead of someone else.

When you create your USP, you should try to keep it to just one sentence, and then put it on everything you print or send out (with the exception of direct mail letters, which we'll cover in a later chapter).

So lets get started creating your USP.

One note about your USP before we get started. You can't be everything to everyone. If you try to be everything to everyone, you end up being nothing to nobody.

Notice how the two examples above didn't try to be everything to everyone? Fedex didn't mention that they had other services, they concentrated on the overnight service.

Dominoes didn't mention anything about pick up service or the best tasting pizzas. They pinpointed the people that wanted pizza delivered hot and fast.

How do you create a USP? Here's some ideas...

Find a need that's going unfulfilled in your area, or even a need that may be being filled in your market, but that no one else is exploiting.

Here's a great example.

How many times have you gone to the doctors office to have to wait 30 minutes in the lobby, then once you're taken back to an examination room, you get to sit half naked on that stupid crackly paper for another 30 minutes before the doctor even comes in to see you?

Now what if you were looking for a new doctor, and you seen an advertisement that used a USP that said: You're guaranteed to see the doctor within 5 minutes of signing in, or we'll pay your insurance copayment".

Do you think that would get your attention if you had a busy lifestyle and didn't have all day to waste at a doctors office?

Michael Gerber, who wrote the E Myth, put it this way. Your USP needs to be a promise that you make to your customers that seems almost impossible to keep, but when you do keep it, it will differentiate you from everyone else that's in your business.

WARNING! Don't adopt a USP that is impossible for you to keep and you can't live up to. This will only backfire on you.

If you have no USP, and make no promises or deliver nothing, that's bad, but if you do make promises and don't keep them, that's much, much worse.

On the following page is a USP worksheet to help you create your USP. Going through and answering all the questions will help you formulate a powerful USP for your restaurant.

Some of the questions you may need to ask your customers. This is very important. When you start asking your customers these questions, and one or two of the answers they give are the same for almost all your customers, you're on to something.

<u>USP Worksheet</u>

Who exactly is your target customer? Describe them in detail. (Mothers, grandmothers, teenagers, business professionals, high school students etc. Be as specific as you can)

_____

_____

_____

_____

_____

_____

What are the three or four most important benefits or results that your customers are wanting from you? (Ask your customers if you're not positive about your answers)

1._____

_____

2._____

_____

3._____

_____

4._____

_____

List three or four specific reasons why your customers do business with you. (Ask your customers this question and see which answers come up the most)

1._____

_____

2._____

_____

3._____

_____

4._____

_____

What's your customers biggest frustration with your competitors?

_____

_____

_____

_____

_____

_____

How can you solve this frustration for them?

_____

_____

_____

_____

_____

_____

What is your guarantee? (refer to section on guarantees)

_____

_____

_____

_____

_____

When you have the above information gathered, can you pinpoint who your customer is, address their frustration, solve it for them, and then back it up with a guarantee? Write your USP below.

_____

_____

_____

_____

_____

_____

Something else to keep in mind when working on your USP. The human brain starts having trouble remembering phrases over seven words long. This was why when the country first started using phone numbers, they kept it to seven digits, for purposes of being able to remember them.

So if you can, try to keep your USP to as close seven words as you can.

Lifetime Value Of A Client

In this section we're going to cover a concept that is absolutely critical to your business. It's called the lifetime value of a client.

Unfortunately, if you ask most restaurant owners how much each one of their customers are worth to them, they will have absolutely no idea.

And the really big problem with that is, that unless we know how much the lifetime value of a client is, we don't know how much to spend to acquire new customers.

Spend, you ask? Yes. You're going to actually "buy" some new customers.

Now we're not going to just hand out cash to random people and ask them to visit your restaurant, but we are going to spend some cash on effective marketing that will bring in new customers.

But unless you know how much one of YOUR customers is "worth" to you, you won't know how much you can afford to spend to get a new customer in the door.

So if a customer was worth – say $100 per year – you wouldn't mind spending $10, or even $20 to get one would you?

Actually – you would probably want to buy as many customers as you could get your hands on – right?

Think of it the same way as you view the stock market. You "invest" $100 into a good stock, then one year later those shares of stock that you invested in returns to you $800 on your initial $100 investment.

So let's look at the chart on the next page and figure out what one of your customers is worth to you on a one year basis.

	2	4	6	8	10	12	14	16	18
$2.00	$4	$8	$12	$16	$20	$24	$28	$32	$36
$3.00	$6	$12	$18	$24	$30	$36	$42	$48	$54
$4.00	$8	$16	$24	$32	$40	$48	$56	$64	$72
$5.00	$10	$20	$30	$40	$50	$60	$70	$80	$90
$6.00	$12	$24	$36	$48	$60	$72	$84	$96	$108
$7.00	$14	$28	$42	$56	$70	$84	$98	$112	$126
$8.00	$16	$32	$48	$64	$80	$96	$112	$128	$144
$9.00	$18	$36	$54	$72	$90	$108	$126	$144	$162
$10.00	$20	$40	$60	$80	$100	$120	$140	$160	$180
$11.00	$22	$44	$66	$88	$110	$132	$154	$176	$198
$12.00	$24	$48	$72	$96	$120	$144	$168	$192	$216
$13.00	$26	$52	$78	**$104**	$130	$156	$182	$208	$234
$14.00	$28	$56	$84	$112	$140	$168	$196	$224	$252
$15.00	$30	$60	$90	$120	$150	$180	$210	$240	$270
$16.00	$32	$64	$96	$128	$160	$192	$224	$256	$288
$17.00	$34	$68	$102	$136	$170	$204	$238	$272	$306
$18.00	$36	$72	$108	$144	$180	$216	$252	$288	$324
$19.00	$28	$76	$114	$152	$190	$228	$266	$304	$342
$20.00	$40	$80	$120	$160	$200	$240	$280	$320	$360
$22.00	$44	$88	$132	$176	$220	$264	$308	$352	$396
$24.00	$48	$96	$144	$192	$240	$288	$336	$384	$432
$26.00	$52	$104	$156	$208	$260	$312	$364	$416	$468
$28.00	$56	$112	$168	$224	$280	$336	$392	$448	$504
$30.00	$60	$120	$180	$240	$300	$360	$420	$480	$540
$32.00	$64	$128	$192	$256	$320	$384	$448	$512	$576
$34.00	$68	$136	$204	$272	$340	$408	$476	$544	$612
$36.00	$72	$144	$216	$288	$360	$432	$504	$576	$648
$38.00	$76	$152	$228	$304	$380	$456	$532	$608	$684
$40.00	$80	$160	$240	$320	$400	$480	$560	$640	$720

If your average sale per customer is $13.00 and they visit you an average of 8 times per year, then you'll make $104.00 per year from each of your clients.

Stick your finger on YOUR average sale (left column). Now move to the right – and stop on YOUR average visits per year. What's the number you came up with? That's the average amount of sales that each of your customers is worth to you on a yearly basis.

Knowing what a customer will spend with you will give you a tremendous advantage over your competitors.

To get an idea of how much a customer is worth to you over a lifetime of owning your business let's take a look at the diagram on the next page.

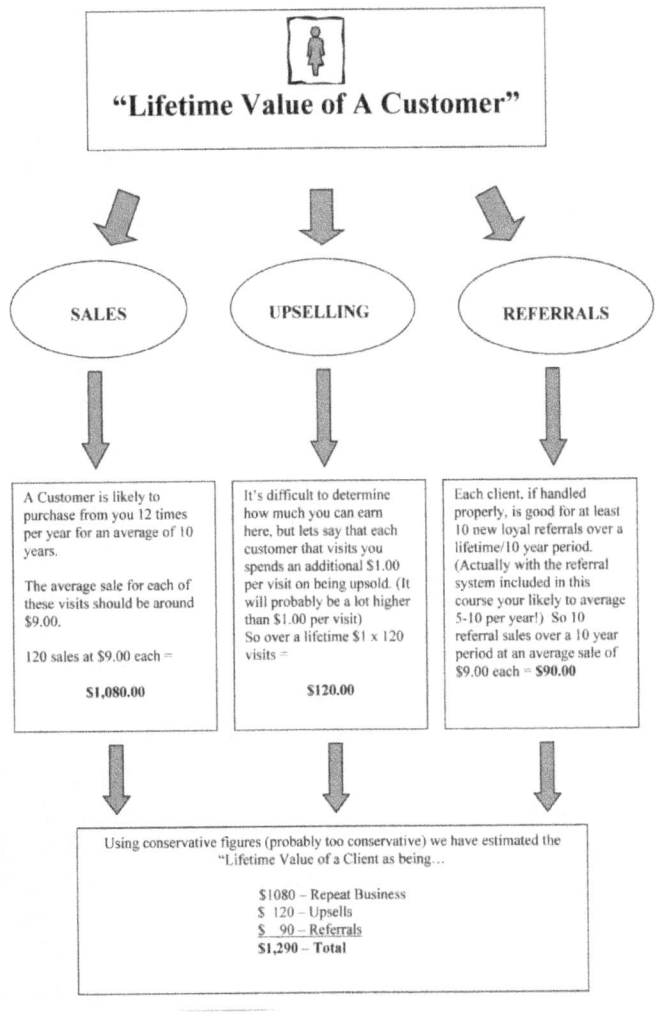

"Lifetime Value of A Customer"

SALES

UPSELLING

REFERRALS

A Customer is likely to purchase from you 12 times per year for an average of 10 years.

The average sale for each of these visits should be around $9.00.

120 sales at $9.00 each =

$1,080.00

It's difficult to determine how much you can earn here, but lets say that each customer that visits you spends an additional $1.00 per visit on being upsold. (It will probably be a lot higher than $1.00 per visit)
So over a lifetime $1 x 120 visits =

$120.00

Each client, if handled properly, is good for at least 10 new loyal referrals over a lifetime/10 year period. (Actually with the referral system included in this course your likely to average 5-10 per year!) So 10 referral sales over a 10 year period at an average sale of $9.00 each = **$90.00**

Using conservative figures (probably too conservative) we have estimated the "Lifetime Value of a Client as being...

$1080 – Repeat Business
$ 120 – Upsells
$ 90 – Referrals
$1,290 – Total

So just by looking at the diagram on the previous page, would it be worth it to spend $10 to get a new customer if they were going to spend $1,290 with you over the next 10 years?

Would it be worth spending $50 or $100 dollars to get that one customer?

Until you know what a client is worth to you per year, you won't have any idea how much to budget to buy new clients and replace the inactive ones.

Most business will focus all their time and advertising money on one thing. New customers! New customers! New customers! And all this time, they neglect the ones that they have.

It's imperative that you realize that your most profitable customer is the <u>one that has already given you money</u>!

There is a gold mine waiting for you in your existing customer list, and I'll show you how to mine that gold with the tactics in this book.

Now how much should you "invest" to acquire a new customer? That's up to you. But think of it this way. Any time it costs you less than their lifetime value to acquire a new customer, you have a profitable business

For example, if you can bring in 10 new prospects for $50.00 ($5 bucks each) and convert just one of them to a "regular" customer, then you can make a lot of cash!

Because based on our example on the previous page, you just spent $50.00 to get one regular customer worth $1,290.

That's a profit of $1,240.00 on your $50.00 investment! Or better yet – it's a return of 2480% on your money!

Now you don't want to spend too little and not get enough clients, but you also don't want to "blindly" spend too much.

Figure out what a client is worth to you, then set a budget that will be enough to acquire them.

I'm going to end this section with a powerful story on how one business seen the lifetime value of a customer, and used that to launch themselves into a multi million dollar company.

You might have seen or heard of the arthritis crème "Icy Hot".

The company that started this brand of arthritis crème was not doing well, so they sold out to another larger company. The new owners of this company were basically going to discontinue the Icy Hot brand, and was just wanting the old companies manufacturing facilities to produce some of their own products in.

Well, shortly after they were to discontinue the Icy Hot brand, they began getting tons of letters and phone calls from little old men and women who had been using this crème for years, and swore by it to relieve their arthritis pain. They were begging them to continue producing Icy Hot.

This company didn't have a lot of money to sink into the Icy Hot brand and get it profitable, but the people that did use it, used it a lot, and were very enthusiastic about it.

Now most other companies out there would have started pouring a ton of money into advertising and marketing to get the brand profitable, but this company had hired an expert marketer named Jay Abraham to help them with their businesses.

Mr. Abraham knew how valuable the lifetime value of a customer is. So he did some research on the Icy Hot brand.

He found that on average, one out of every two people that bought one of the jars of Icy Hot, because it worked so well, would usually buy 10 more jars over the next 12 months.

At the time, each of these jars sold for $3.00 each. So every time they acquired a new customer, he discovered that over the next 12 months, that customer was worth about $25.00 in net profit after manufacturing expenses.

So what Mr. Abraham did, was he went to thousands of different radio stations, newspapers, magazines, television studios, and tons of other advertising mediums, and he told them.

"Look, if you'll advertise our Icy Hot product in your medium, we'll let you keep 100% of the profit on everything you sell."

A lot of these newspapers and radio stations thought he was crazy! Every time they sold one of the $3.00 jars of Icy Hot through their form of advertising, they got to keep all $3.00. Mr. Abraham didn't even ask for the cost of manufacturing the product!

Think about this… That would be like you going to your local newspaper and saying "If you'll advertise my pizzeria in your newspaper, every time a customer sees your ad, comes to my restaurant and buys a pizza, I'll give you all the money I receive from that customer for that pizza." Sounds crazy doesn't it, but there's a genius to what Mr. Abraham was doing.

The only stipulation that Mr. Abraham had was that whenever an order came in, the customers name and address was promptly given to the Icy Hot company so they could get the order out quickly and make sure the customer was satisfied.

Once they had the name and address of someone that bought Icy Hot, they would internally advertise to those people, reminding them to order more Icy Hot, and marketing some of their other products.

This strategy brought in thousands of new customers. And since the cost for them to manufacture and ship each jar of Icy Hot only cost them 45 cents, each time they acquired a new customer, they were basically trading 45 cents for $25.00.

The Icy Hot brands sales immediately shot through the roof.

How much?

They grew from $20,000 in sales to **13 Million dollars** in sales in only 18 months!

This is the power of knowing what the lifetime value of your customers is.

<u>Herd Database</u>

Back in the wild west days, ranchers made their living from their herd. They took great care to make sure that their herd grew and prospered. This was how they made their living.

If the rancher had a large herd, chances are he had a decent income. However, if the rancher only had a small herd, then he was probably struggling to make ends meet.

However large the herd was though, it absolutely had to be fed and taken care of, or the herd would die off, leaving no revenue for the rancher.

Your data base is just like the ranchers herd. The larger your data base is, the more revenue you will bring in. But most importantly, you <u>must</u> take care of your herd or they will wander off to greener pastures.

To take care of your herd, you must have some kind of data base that tracks your customers. I can't imagine trying to run any type of business without having a detailed customer list of everyone that has bought from me.

Still, there are thousands of pizzeria owners out there that will look completely lost when you ask them if they have a customer list. And the few that do keep some type of customer list, rarely, if ever, use them.

This is like trying to swim with cinderblocks tied to your feet. And we all know what happens to people that are forced to go swimming with cinderblocks.

I was talking to another pizzeria owner who had a store a few towns away from mine. He did a promotion that grabbed my attention. He ran a $2.99 large pepperoni special for pickup only, from 11am to 5pm on one Saturday in June, with a limit of 3 pizzas per person.

He had a banner made up to advertise it in front of his store, and staffed heavily the day the promotion ran. He was pretty happy with the results too. He told me he almost 300 people place orders that day using that promotion.

I told him that was a really good idea for a promotion, and then asked him if he got everyone's name, address, and phone number that got the $2.99 pizzas…. He didn't.

But he assured me that he knew most of those people would come back and order again.

How does he know they will come back? The truth of the matter is he doesn't, and since he's not tracking his customers, he has no idea if selling those pizzas at a loss will win him any sales in the future.

He had a great idea, but completely blew it when he didn't add all those people to his herd. By simply getting their contact information, he could have mailed them an offer if they hadn't ordered again within 30 days.

I can't over emphasize how important your data base is to you. It's an absolute must, that you get every customers name, address, and phone number. Then track how much they buy, and how often.

Think about it this way. If every customer in your data base orders once per month, and has an average order of $18.00 per visit, then each customer is worth $216 per year to you.

What if ten of those customers stopped ordering from you, and started ordering from one of your competitors? That's $2,160 that was just stolen out of your pockets by one of your competitors.

What would you do if someone got your credit card number and bought $2,160 worth of stuff, or went to an atm machine and withdrew $2,160? You would go nuts!

You would demand the person go to jail, and return every penny they took from you.

However when a pizzeria owner loses a customer and $216 every year doesn't get deposited into his bank account, he hardly thinks twice about it.

And that's if he even realizes that he's losing customers!

Most owners unknowingly let their customer base slowly dwindle away, and then wonder what happened when they're on the edge of financial ruin.

From now on, you will know who has stopped ordering from you, and when they do, you will work to get them back.

To track your customers, you don't need anything too expensive. Most all of the Point of Sale systems out there today have a customer data base that will do the job.

I used Rapidfire all the way up until I sold my store. It was a dinosaur by todays standards, but did exactly what I needed it to do.

I could capture the name, address, and phone numbers of everyone that ordered. I could tell what day and what time they ordered. I could tell when their last order was, and how much money they spent with me.

If someone hadn't ordered from me in 30 days, that was a signal to send them some kind of offer to get them to order again. If it was over 60 days, I needed to get more aggressive with the offer to get them back in the door. If over 90 days, something was wrong. I would usually send them a letter for a free medium pizza to get them back in the door, then ask them why they hadn't ordered in so long.

If you don't have a way of capturing your customers names and tracking them, you need to find a way. Finding a used Pos system for a couple thousand bucks would pay for itself in only a few short months.

There are also several different types of software that you could purchase and load on a computer to do this. Quickbooks has a point of sale software program that would do the trick.

Just be sure to make it a priority to capture your customers information from this day forward.

Raising Prices

If you use only one strategy out of this entire course, you absolutely need to use this one. This one strategy will make a huge difference in your business.

Most independent pizza owners are terrified of raising their prices. This is mostly due to a huge psychological barrier that stands in the way of raising them.

The important thing to know though is that the psychological barrier is in the mind of the business owner, not the customers!

By raising prices, you will quickly add more profit to your pizza store. I know this sounds incredibly simple, but once again, most business owners are terrified to raise their prices.

They immediately think that if they raise their prices higher than their competitors, that their customers will stop buying from them. This simply isn't the case. There have been numerous studies done, and they all show that people rarely buy on price, and actually, price is one of the least important things when customers are making a decision of who to buy from.

I know a lot of people will point to Wal-Mart and say see... they compete on price, and look how successful they are.

And you're right, right now Wal-Mart is very successful because of their prices, but I would venture to say that might not be the case within the next 20 years.

Look back at the other big retail stores that have tried to use price as their main buying point to customers. There was Montgomery Ward, they are no longer in business, there was Sears, they almost went bankrupt and just managed to survive, and right before Wal-Mart began taking the lead as price king, there was K-Mart.

So if a new competitor was to arise tomorrow, and have all their merchandise at half the price that Wal-Mart does, do you think Wal-Mart would still be able to hold on to as many sales as they have now?

Maybe, maybe not. But see how risky using low prices are to your business? You might be the lowest price one day, and the next day you're not. So what do you use for your slogan then? Lowest price somedays?

If everyone bought just on price, we would all be driving around in tiny cheap cars, and living in inexpensive one bedroom apartments. Engagement rings would be imitation gold with fake diamonds, and no one would be wearing name brand clothes.

You've probably heard the passage from the Bible… "if you live by the sword, you die by the sword" well, if you live by price, you will die by price. If you're trying to compete with the big chain stores based on price alone, you're going to die a slow painful death.

I've seen the big chain stores drop prices so low that you would swear that they were losing money with each sale they make. And there's a really good possibility that they are.

But by dropping prices that low, and having the deep pockets that they do it's simply a matter of time before the small pizza shops go under trying to compete with them based on price.

This is a tactic that if you keep your eyes peeled you will see happen in a lot of businesses where there are large chains. They simply move into a new area, drop prices so low that the little guys go out of business, then bring their prices back up after they have eliminated their competition.

Think this doesn't ever happen? Watch the next time a large chain store opens up in your neighborhood. They'll leave their prices high when they first open because everyone will be trying them out because they are new in town.

But then, they will drop prices to where they are breaking even, or even taking a small loss, to get all the business in the area. And if this happens in your neighborhood, there's no way you can drop your prices with them and think you can wait them out.

It's simply a matter of attrition. They have the cash to take a loss for several years if needed. You probably have the cash to last a few months if you're lucky.

Don't try to compete on price-you will lose! After finishing this book you'll know how to compete with the big chain stores, and price won't be an issue.

When you raise your prices, one of three things are going to happen. Your sales will go up, your sales will go down, or your sales will stay the same.

Your sales will go up: As incredible as this may sound, there is a possibility that your sales will actually go up when you raise your prices. This is due to price psychology.

If you wanted to go out and purchase the best watch on the market, what's the first thing you would look at? Price! Its human nature, it's programmed into us. If we want the best of anything, the first that we look at is price.

Take two pizzas from two different stores. Both stores order their food supplies from the same distributor. One charges 19.99 for a large pizza, the other charges $5.99 for basically the same pizza.

If you were going to take someone that you had just started dating out for pizza, which pizza would you buy for them? If you bought them the $5.99 pizza, you would run a risk of being thought of as cheap, even though both pizzas are made the same, the one that is selling for $5.99 has a perceived worth of only $5.99!

Can you see where this is going? You're the one who decides how your pizza is perceived based on the price that you put on it.

Now you obviously can't buy the cheapest ingredients possible, then skimp on the cheese and toppings and charge a high price for it and have people not find you out.

Here's a great example of the perceived value of an item based on price.

Lets look at women's underwear for a second, shall we? (don't act like that didn't get your attention)

You can go to almost any department store and get a basic cotton pair of underwear for about $1.34 per pair. These have a really low perceived value.

Now this same pair of cotton underwear will cost you over $5.00 per pair at Victoria's Secret. These are perceived as having a little bit more value than the $1.34 pair, however their both made out of the exact same material.

Let's go even further. Above the Victoria's Secret underwear, there's the Australian Wicked Weasel brand panty that sells for $15.46 each. That's over 1000% higher than the basic pair you can get out of a retail or department store! Same cotton panty as the other two, but a much higher perceived value.

And if that difference in price doesn't blow your mind, for the same basic item, you can go to www.nancymeyer.com and check out the Carine Gilson Silk and Lace Shorty for the everyday low price of only $448.00! Granted, it's not made out of cotton like the other pairs, but it's not plated in gold either, it's just a lace panty!

Same basic item, huge difference in perceived value. What if Nancy Meyer had listed the price on their panty at 19.99 each instead of the $448? You wouldn't have jumped online as soon as you read about them and checked them out would you? (don't act like you didn't set this course down to go look at them online)

Same thing with your pizza. Most people think that the more expensive something is, the better it is, so your marketplace will end up taking you at your own appraisal.

Raising prices <u>can</u> actually end up increasing your sales.

Your sales will go down: The other thing that can happen is that your sales go down. More than likely, you will have a few of the bottom feeding coupon clippers that will get mad if you raise prices and jump ship.

These are the customers you probably don't want anyway, and probably would have bailed to one of your competitors the first time they got a coupon in the mail for $2.00 off a large pizza.

The fact of the matter is that if you just raised your prices by a tiny 10%, you could lose up to 10% of your customers, and still have almost the same amount of sales as you did before raising your prices.

This means that if you had 5000 customers in your data base, you could lose 500 of them because of the 10% price increase, but do you really think that 500 of your customers would leave you because of such a small increase?

When I raised prices by a buck per pizza, I had only two people complain about it, no one else even blinked when we told them their totals. It's like they didn't even realize what the price of the pizza was before the price increase.

Actually, let's take a quick quiz and see if we know how much other business charge for their products.

How much does a gallon of milk cost at your local grocery store? What about a box of laundry detergent at your local retailer? How much is Burger King charging for a large milkshake? How about your local burger restaurant, how much do they get for one of their hamburgers?

Could you name the exact price off the top of your head for any of those items? Probably not. That's because most people don't know what your prices are, and if you make tiny increments, they're not going to notice them.

Now you can't make a jump from $9.99 to $15.99 and think no one will notice, but most people won't notice you going from $9.99 to 10.99.

Your sales will stay the same: This is most likely what will happen when you raise your prices. Most people won't even notice the price increase, and will go about doing business with you as normal.

If you have just raised your sales by 10%, and your sales stay the same, you have just added a huge amount of money to your bottom line. How much? Let's take a look.

To keep the numbers simple, let's say you have 1000 regular customers, ordering once per month, with an average ticket of $20.00

1000 customers x $20.00 = $20,000 per month

Now by raising prices only 10%, our average order now becomes $22.00 per month.
1000 customers x 22.00 = $22,000 per month

That's an instant $2000 profit every month! That's an additional **$24,000 in profit every year!** What could you do with an extra $24,000 every year in practically free money?

See how profitable this can be? You absolutely need to do this. Implement this as soon as you get done reading this page, it's that important to your bottom line.

It's strange to me when I see someone buy an existing business and the first thing they do is drop the prices that the previous owner had. I've seen this firsthand when I first put my store up for sale.

I had a woman who was very interested in purchasing my store and had flown down from the state of Washington to take a look at the store and possibly sign contracts for the sale.

While we were sitting down at lunch, discussing terms and such, I asked her how she planned on marketing the store. Very first words out of her mouth were…. "I'm going to cut prices".

So here is a woman who has done (as far as I know) no real market research on the area. Didn't ask any customers if they thought the prices were to high. And didn't have any other real marketing plan other than cutting prices!

At the end of the day, she couldn't decide if she wanted to sign an agreement and put money down on the store. Even though I wanted to sell my store, I told her that if she wasn't 100% sure, then she shouldn't buy.

If she had purchased the store, she was going to cut prices by $2.00 per pizza. That's like taking a job and telling your boss… I would much rather work for $9.00 per hour than $19.00 per hour.

When I purchased my store, here's what my menu pricing looked like.

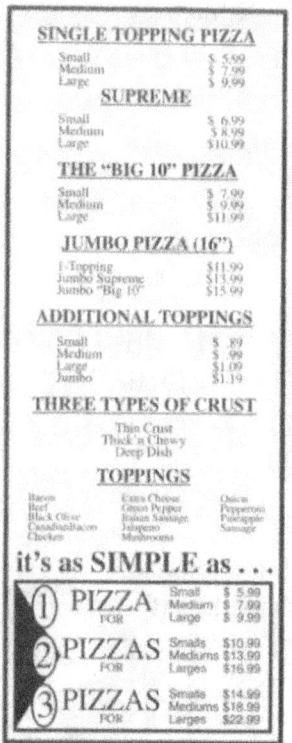
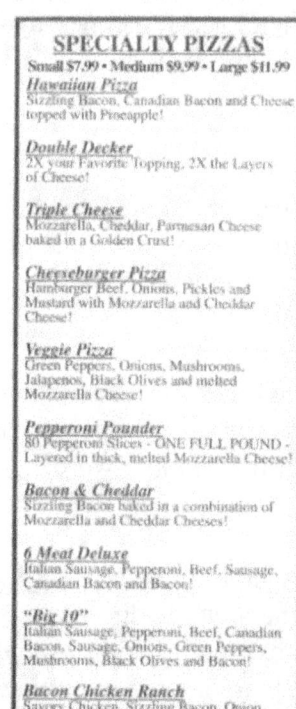
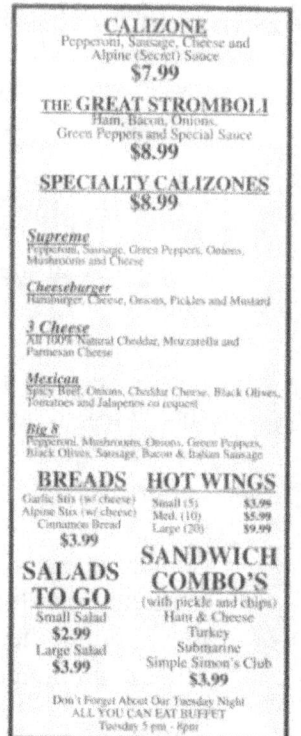

Really boring menu, cheap pricing. Notice how it's easy to see the prices? This is how you <u>do not</u> want to make your menu.

Now here's a copy of my menu right before I sold my store.

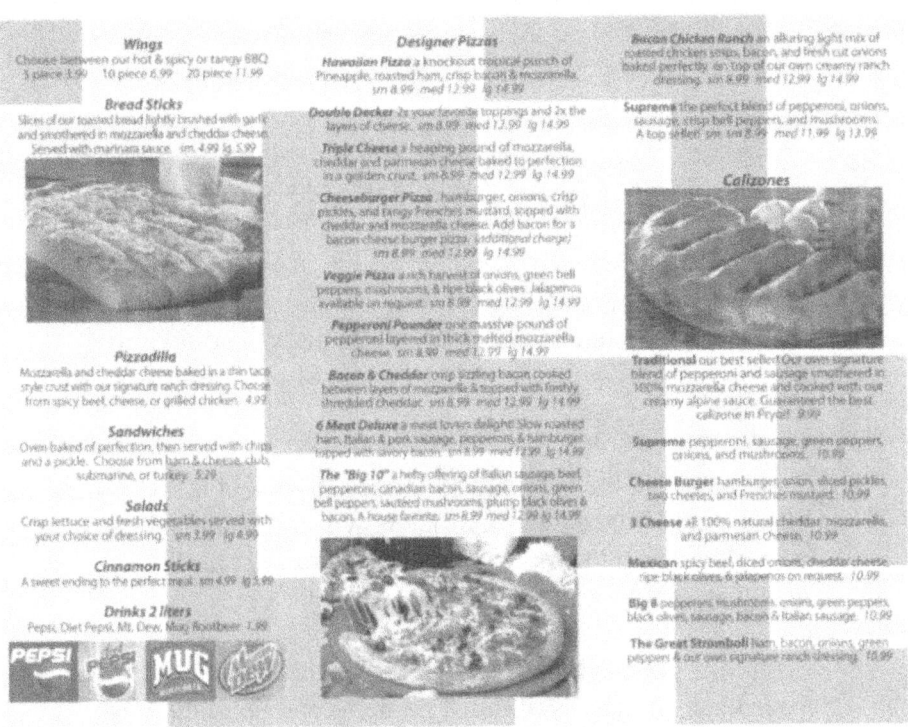

The prices on this menu have been raised and are "hidden" in the description of the pizza. Also notice how the descriptions are much more appetizing than the original menu, and the addition of full color photos increased sales even more.

Direct Mail Letters

Direct mail letters will be one of the main weapons in your arsenal. These letters are so effective that if I could only use one type of advertising for the rest of my life, it would be these direct mail letters.

To get started, the first thing we need to look at is the envelope. A lot of other marketers will tell you the most important thing to worry about is the letter itself. I disagree. And for this reason.

 If no one opens your envelope, it doesn't matter how good your letter or offer is, it's just going to end up in the trash.

To help you understand why this is so important, we're going to use the lecture used by the late Gary Halbert, who was probably the greatest direct response marketer in the world.

Gary said that America sorts its mail into two stacks. There's the A pile, and there's the B pile. Gary also said that America sorts their mail into these two piles while standing over the trash can.

The A pile is mail that will be kept and opened. This is usually bills and personal letters from friends. The B pile is what goes right into the trash. This is usually blatant junk mail that contains a sales pitch.

When you sort through your mail, what do you usually do with something that is in a bright yellow envelope with "Very Urgent" across the front or "Act now to get 20% off Time magazine" across the back?

Well if you're like me, it goes right into the trash without being opened. Same thing with all these bank and insurance envelopes. You know the ones I'm talking about, the "Pre- Approved" and the "Lower Rates Inside" envelopes.

They usually have their logos stamped in bright colors on the envelope as well. All these are what's known as "teaser copy", and lets us know right away that there's a sales pitch inside. These all go straight into the B pile.

Sometimes... just sometimes a piece of B pile mail will be kept if the envelope looks interesting enough, then maybe... just maybe if you remember it later on, and you don't have anything else to do, you might just open it.

Now let's look at the A pile. This pile is usually made up of the bills and personal letters. What would you do if you received a plain white envelope that had your name and address hand written in blue ink, and an actual live first class stamp in the upper right hand corner?

You wouldn't just automatically throw it into the trash. You would open it to at least see who it's from.

By leaving your logo off, using an actual first class stamp, and handwriting the address in blue ink, you have a much better chance of getting your direct mail piece opened.

In the upper left side of the envelope, you should only put you're actual return address. Don't put your name or company name there. This provokes curiosity, and the recipient will be more likely to open the letter to see who it's from.

Everyone <u>always</u> opens their personal mail. So if we get our sales letter into the A pile so it actually gets opened, then we have met our first objective.

Now here's where things could get tricky.

If you're mailing out 20,000 or 30,000 letters, there's obviously no way you're going to be handwriting that many addresses.

The best way to handle this is to have your printer print up the number of envelopes you need with <u>just your return address</u> in the upper left hand corner. Remember, no company name here.

If you're using a mailing house, and I would recommend using one if you're mailing out any kind of volume at all, have them print the customers name and address on the envelope so it looks like the address has been typed on, or see if they can put the address on using a handwriting font, using blue ink. This will probably cost you a little bit more, but is definitely worth the small added expense. **Never** use "current resident" or "dear occupant". This makes the letter look impersonal. Always use the customers name, and never use those stick on address labels regardless of how large or small your mailing is going to be.

Now we get to using stamps. Your mailing house can get you bulk rate pricing and meter the envelope for you, but this once again doesn't look personal. The other option is to use a bulk rate stamp.

This stamp doesn't look like a first class stamp, but would be much better than using metered mail.

I would go with the bulk rate stamp every time, unless you're doing small mailings, in which case I would use a first class stamp with the handwritten address.

If you use a mailing house to stuff, stamp, and address your envelopes, that's fine.

However – **Never** let the mailing house drop your letters at the post office!

Why you ask? It's simply good math for the mailing house to stuff and stamp only 90% of your mail then it is to stuff and stamp 100% of your mail.

Now surely this isn't happening to your mailings – after all, they showed you a receipt from the post office showing the number of pieces of mail they dropped off at the post offices loading dock.

And receipts never lie… Especially when their signed by a competent employee of the United States Federal Government…right?

This is how it actually plays out…

Imagine a guy named bob who works at the loading dock for the post office. There's something you should know about ol' Bob. He's got five kids, a wife that nags the holy crap out of him, one more kid on the way that his wife doesn't know about yet, (if you get my drift), a twelve year old car that he's been driving around with the spare donut tire for the past two weeks, a kitchen table full of overdue bills, and he has the hots for one of his little co-workers known as Rhonda the Honda.

Rhonda isn't too particular about her guy friends as long as they come equipped with their own personal pharmacy.

Anyways, our pal Bob has all this going through his mind when the truck from your friendly mailing house shows up with your letters, driven by the mail house owner, Jon.

Jon backs his truck up to the dock, approaches Bob, and the conversation goes something like this...

Jon: Hey Bob, how's it goin? Get laid lately?

Bob: Naa, just the wife, I'd sure like to get back into Rhonda the Hondas pants again, but you know how Rhonda is... no blow, no go.

Jon: That's too bad... Hey, that reminds me, I've got something here for you. Its pure Columbian flake, man. Good f$%#ing s#@t man!

Bob: Awesome man... You're alright! You just saved my cojones from another week of the same ol' same ol'!

Jon: Not a problem man, glad to help you out. Hey listen, I need to get a receipt for this mail I'm dropping off. I'm not sure how it's gonna weigh out on the scales, but it's supposed to weight out to about 80,000 pieces, and that's what I need a receipt for, you dig?

Bob: No problem pal, just have your guys throw those letters in the cart over there and I'll get that receipt for you right away!

And so Jon drops off 60,000 or 70,000 pieces of mail, gets a receipt for 80,000 pieces of mail, and let's face it... how are you ever going to know this happened. And if you even suspect it, how are you going to prove it?

Cold hard fact... You can't!

I've experienced this myself. I had my mail shop mail out 6500 postcards with a pretty good two pizza offer on them. How many of those postcards did I have redeemed?

ZERO!

I called the mailing house and asked them if they had been dropped off at the post office yet. They said "yep, three days ago".

A few days later I called them again. This time they told me that since I mailed them bulk rate, (another mistake I made) it would probably take the post office a few extra days to get them out.

One week later. They tell me that they dropped them off at the post office and would fax me over a receipt showing this (refer to the story I just told you). They actually had the cojones to tell me that maybe my ad was so bad that no one responded....

Now admittedly, I'm not the greatest copy writer in the world, but I've NEVER had a zero response from a mailing. NEVER!

And what's even stranger, is I mailed one to myself and never received it.

That's another tip, always mail to yourself, this is another way of seeing if your mailing is bad, or if the mail didn't go out.

So I start asking the people that work for me if they received one of the postcards in the mail. At that time there were approximately 12 of my employees that lived in the city limits that should have received the postcard.

None of them had received it. Some of them called their friends and relatives to ask if they had received it. Nada… not one person out of about 30 that we contacted received the postcard.

So after fighting with the mail house over this, they finally told me… "Look, we dropped off your mailing at the post office and sent you a receipt, you'll have to take it up with them."

Needless to say I found a new mailing house to do business with.

So I go tromping into the post office, armed with my receipt from the mail house.

And being the experts in great customer service that the U.S. Postal Service is known for, the conversation went something like this.

"Hi, I had my mailing house drop off some postcards here a few weeks ago, see here's my receipt, but I don't think any of them got delivered, can you check on that for me?"

The response I was kind of expecting was <u>at the very least</u> "sure, let me check on that for you."

However that's not what I got from the overweight postal clerk who sat behind his counter with a smug look on his face.

"If they dropped it off, we got it delivered" he told me.

"Well" I responded, "I mailed one to myself, and to almost a dozen of my employees, and none of us received one of them".

"We always deliver all the mail we get" was his answer, still with that smug look on his face.

It was almost like he was trained to say those exact same lines no matter what proof I showed him. Kinda like when a soldier is caught and interrogated, they only give their name, rank, and serial number, even if they're tortured.

The only way I was going to be able to torture this guy was to dangle a twinkie in front of him just out of reach, but since I didn't have a twinkie, I asked to talk to the manager of that office.

Basically he told me that <u>sometimes</u> mail might <u>accidentally</u> get thrown away if the postal employee doesn't feel like delivering it. And he would be happy to file a complaint for me if I could show him proof that the postcards got thrown away.

So basically I could drop the whole thing and chalk it up as a learning experience, or I could start scowering all the dumpsters in the city limits hoping to locate 6500 postcards.

And even if I did get lucky enough to find the postcards, I needed someone to have actually seen the postman physically throw the postcards into the dumpster to file a complaint.

So I took this as a learning experience and found a better way of mailing letters.

First, I always pick up my mail personally from the mail house after they have addressed and stamped them. I <u>never</u> let them drop them at the post office.

Next, I personally drop the mail off at the post office myself. Usually on a Wednesday or Thursday so the letter hits on a Friday.

Never under any circumstances drop your letters off on a Friday after 3:00 pm!

The postal employees being the over achievers that they are, want to get off work and out the door asap on Fridays. They can't do this until all the mail received is put in its proper place for distribution, or… it's out of sight.

Out of sight meaning stuffed in a corner somewhere until Monday.

And you don't want your mail hitting on a Saturday or Monday anyways, so never mail on a Friday.

Another tip. If you're doing a large mailing, never drop them off at the same post office.

If they notice that you're dropping off a large quantity of letters, there's a chance that they may end up in the dumpster and not get delivered. This is even if you're using a first class stamp on all of them.

They figure that if it's a large quantity mailing, you're not going to follow up on each letter and call everyone you mailed to and see if they received it.

So just to be safe, if I'm doing several thousand letters at one time, I'll drop around 500 letters at four different post offices, or at the least, 1000 at two different offices.

It might sound like I'm going overboard using all this caution, but you have to remember that every letter that you mail could be costing you about 50 cents each, and if they don't get delivered, not only are you out the 50 cents, you also missing out on the sale it might have brought you.

If you don't believe me that this kinda stuff happens, run a test yourself.

Mail 5000 letters by just dropping them off at the mail house, and mail 5000 letters using the steps I described.

Use something in the letter to let you know which is which, such as a different phone number for them to call in on, or asking them to use a certain coupon code.

You'll find out that the mail that you deliver to the post office yourself will constantly have a larger response then the mail left at the mailing house.

So now that we have all the technical stuff out of the way on how to mail your letter, let's get to writing it.

A.I.D.A.

Like I said before, if there was only one marketing vehicle that I could use for the rest of my life in any type of business, it would be the personal sales letter.

Personal sales letters are just that… personal. <u>People want to do business with a person, not a company</u>. Remember that, write it down, it's extremely important.

When you send someone a personal letter, it gives them that "warm and fuzzy" feeling. That feeling that someone thinks they're important enough for you to actually sit down and take the time to write them a letter. You won't get that from the big chain stores.

You'll also notice that after your mailings, that one of the first things a lot of people will say when calling in an order or visiting is "I got a letter from Paul saying that I get such and such for free," or "Paul sent me a letter saying I get this special price."

The reason they do this is because the letter makes them feel important. I mean hey… they got this personal letter from the store owner with this great offer. No other business owners have sent them a personal letter.

I'm not going to go into great depth on how to write a sales letter. There are hundreds of books on the subject, and there would simply be too much information to cover and it would take up most of this book. I will touch on the basics of writing one though, and then show you a fast "cheat" method to getting around spending hours trying create and write your letter.

Now when writing your letter, there's a basic formula that you should follow. It's the A.I.D.A. formula.

You have to capture their <u>attention</u>, you've got to catch their <u>interest</u>, you've got to arouse their <u>desire</u> (sounds dirty doesn't it), and you have to call them to <u>action</u>.

<u>A</u>ttention

<u>I</u>nterest

<u>D</u>esire

<u>A</u>ction

Now while the layout of the letter is important, the most important thing to remember is that your letter doesn't have to be perfect, it just has to be good enough. I've been guilty of doing this myself. I'll write a letter, but it's not quite perfect.

I'll go back and change some things… not quite perfect yet. Go back and tweak it a little bit more… still not good enough. One month later, I'm still changing things when I could have had it mailed and some revenue coming in.

A few things to keep in mind when writing your letters. Don't write big paragraphs. If you write your letters with big paragraphs your reader will take one look at the letter and throw it in the trash. It will just look like it's too much work to read.

Remember the last time you had to read some legal form or warranty agreement with tons of text just all stacked together. How did you feel when you looked at it knowing you had to read it? Did it look like a lot of work? Did it look daunting?

If your letter looks like that, your customer doesn't have to read it, and they won't. It will simply go into the waste basket without another thought.

Instead, break your paragraphs up into a few sentences each. You can even use one sentence if you like. Just don't use one sentence per paragraph for the whole letter. This is what's called eye relief.

On the next page is an example of a letter with good eye relief, and with bad eye relief.

You be the judge... if Simple Simons Pizza isn't the Best Pizza You've ever had,
I'll give you your money back – every penny!
PLUS – I'll give you a
FREE Medium One Topping Pizza
And FREE Delivery when you buy any Large Designer Pizza!

Dear neighbor,

Tired of having to order thirty or forty dollars worth of pizza to be able to use a coupon for a measly couple of bucks off of your order? Are you frustrated with paying three and four dollar delivery fees, just to have your pizza delivered by a rude delivery driver who could care less how long you have to wait for your pizza?

Finally – you and your family can get Great Tasting Simple Simons Pizza – Delivered right to your home – For FREE!

Unlike others – we don't charge a three dollar delivery fee, give the driver a dollar of it, and then keep the rest to make up for any coupons you may have used.

Our Professional delivery drivers work for tips, so its in their best interest to make sure your pizza arrives to your home piping hot, and as fast as possible.

So while everyone else dishes out that "budget taste" and screams for your money, my proposition is simple. Order a Large Designer Pizza – and I'll include a Medium One Topping Pizza – FREE.

You'll get two great pizzas – and for less than you'd spend on mass produced ordinary pizza put together on frozen dough disks.

But, the Special Treatment doesn't stop there –

I put my neck on the line with every order –If you should ever be disappointed – for any reason, please let me know. If I cant make it right – I'll give you your money back – every penny!

Check out the menu I sent you, pick out the two pizzas that get your taste buds watering – then give us a call. Our phone number is 825-5500.

You'll get fast, FREE delivery right to your front door – or you can pick up. You'll find us at 125 Steve Berry Blvd. – right across the street from Wal Mart.

Hope to see you soon – sincerely,

Paul Baker

P.S. Please – take us up on this offer tonight! But definitely before this letter expires in three weeks. The FREE Medium Topping pizza is yours – and as always – if you're not 100% satisfied, your money back – every penny!

If our pizza isn't better than the fast food guys...
We'll give you're your money back!
PLUS
Not only is this offer risk free – but I've also decided to throw in a
FREE order of cheese sticks, FREE 2 liter of Pepsi,
And FREE Delivery* when you order any large Designer pizza!

Dear Friend,

There's a few things you should know about pizza.
We start off at 7:30 every morning making fresh pizza dough with our 1979 hobart mixer (yes that's the year it was made). We round all our doughballs by hand, and place them in the cooler for them to proof. We constantly keep a close eye on them for the next few hours, and when they are perfect, we use one for your pizza. We cut all the vegetables by hand. We have real bacon – not some imitation bacon bit. And our pepperoni is top quality.

Between screaming about being the fastest, the cheapest, and the cheesiest, the big guys forgot about something. You – the discriminating customer. You want the best – and they don't have it. Never did.

Did you know that a lot of pizza places use powdered pizza sauce? Just add hot water and stir. Some even put grease in their dough so it will last forever. And some even put lard in their pizza pans before cooking so the crust will deep fry and stay crispy.

And don't you want to laugh when you see that some places are charging a three and four dollar delivery fee (you don't think the driver actually gets to keep that do you?) Oh... and most of their "coupon" prices are actually their everyday prices – they just put them on a coupon so you'll think your saving money. Your not.

Well... it's a little embarrassing but ... if your looking for a perfectly round pizza? We might not be able to help you. Since everything is made by hand, including rolling the dough and hand stretching it, well...

... lets just say they're not perfectly round "punched" out things you get from the big guys.! Just look at our pizzas! Our Big 16 pizza has six different meats, and four different vegetables on it. Our Bacon Chicken Ranch uses real bacon and tender white meat chicken. The Hawaiian has a quarter pound of hand sliced pineapples! You can have your pizza custom made – the way you want it!

Well...it will be dinner time soon. Hurry down here...(offer ends November 30th) and savor the best pizza you've ever had! We're located at 125 Steve Berry Blvd, right across the street from Wal Mart. And if you want to call in for carry out, or FREE delivery, our phone number is 825-5500.

Don't forget about our Ultimate Guarantee. I put my neck on the line with every order – If you should ever be disappointed – for any reason, please let me know. If I cant make it right – I'll give you your money back – every penny! If you decide to purchase your pizza from any of our competitors here in Pryor, and are just not happy with the pizza you received, bring in the uneaten portion, and I'll replace it with one of ours – for FREE!

Hope to see you soon – sincerely,

Notice how much easier to read the letter on the left is.
You can take in the information in short easy gulps. Notice
how this book is written, several sentences then a break.
Just by taking a glance at the letter on the right, you might
automatically assume that it's just too much work to read.
The letter on the left is much easier on the eyes, and
appears like a quick easy read.

If you have a lot of information to put in your letters, just
keep adding more pages, don't reduce the type size and
pack as much as you can onto one page, you'll kill your
response rate by doing so.

The length of your letter isn't too important, it just needs to be interesting. You can't bore people into a sale. Most of my personal letters for pizza were only one page, sometimes two.

I have seen some direct sales advertisers send out 18-29 page sales letters with excellent results. Keep this in mind, the more you tell, the more you sell. It's one of the basic rules of direct response marketing.

If your letter starts getting into several pages you might want to consider using headers. These are small headlines that break up the letter even more, and pull the eyes attention.

If you have a four page letter, and on the second page there's a header, the reader subconsciously only thinks they have to read up to that header, then they can quit reading, or continue. It works almost like a chapter in a book, and draws the readers attention.

Here are two pages from a letter I wrote for a charity I'm involved with. The letter was over five pages long, and started to look like a lot of work to read.

You Can Win $100 Of FREE Vitamins Just For Taking A Stand Against Child Sex Trafficking Here In Pryor!

Dear John,

Hi, my name is Paul Baker, I used to own the Simple Simons Pizza right here in Pryor, and I have an important story that I need to share with you about a girl named Megan (not her real name). **I need to warn you though**, this story does have some graphic details, so you probably don't want to leave this letter lying around where young kids can read it.

Anyways, this girl Megan that I'm telling you about was 15 years old when these events took place. She was playing in her front yard when two men pulled up and asked her for directions. When she approached the vehicle, they dragged her inside, and taped her mouth, eyes and hands. This happened in broad daylight.

Megan was taken several hours away to an apartment complex, where the two men told Megan that they were going to kill her. They would put a gun to her head and ask her if she wanted to be shot in the head or the chest. She said that when she didn't answer, she could hear them pulling the hammer on the gun back while the cold metal barrel was against her head, then she felt the trigger pulled and the loud click of the hammer coming down. Her captors would laugh each time after doing this, telling her that this time the gun was really loaded.

Megans captors then raped her, and forced her into a dog kennel so small that she had to lay on her back with her knees tucked almost up to her chest. She was kept in that kennel for several days and was forced to eat dog biscuits for her meals. When she was finally let out of the cage several days later, she was drugged, and then gang raped by five men that showed up at the apartment.

Later that same night, the two men drove Megan around town trying to sell her. When they were unsuccessful they took her back to the apartment and forced her back into the kennel. Megan was subject to all kinds of abuses and torture from her captors.

Within a few days after arriving at the apartment, an ad was placed on craigs list, and she had men coming at all hours of the day and night demanding sex from her. If she refused, she was beaten. For almost 40 days, Megan was beaten, raped, and forced to have sex of the most degrading kind, but because her captors threatened to kill her and her family, she didn't dare attempt to escape.

Megan was eventually found by the Phoenix police department. They found her tied up and crushed in a drawer under the bed. It actually took the police two searches of the small apartment to find Megan because the drawers under the bed were so small that just by looking at them, you wouldn't think that a person could fit in one. One of the officers happened to hear movement from the drawer when he walked by and discovered Megan stuffed inside. When she was pulled out of the drawer, she was so weak and malnourished that she couldn't stand under her own strength.

The Average Lifespan Of A Sex Trafficked Victim Here In Oklahoma Is Only Four Years. Most Of These Children Die From STDs, Violence, Or Exhaustion.

Read that again…That's right, that's the average life span here in Oklahoma. In fact, Oklahoma is now one of the top ten destinations for child sex trafficking in the world! And the average age of these children forced into sex trafficking is only twelve years old!

And don't think that these scumbag traffickers put any kind of age limit on who their willing to sell. In fact—one child trafficker told an undercover shared hope international agent "If you pay the price, you can get what you want, and I can get it for you. Now if you want something really young, that $200, it's just going to cost you a little bit more than that."

When these children finally are rescued or manage to escape, their lives have been completely shattered. When they are found, they usually have nothing on them, no identification (the traffickers take it from them), no personal belongings, and usually just the one set of cloths that the trafficker makes them wear. The physical, mental and spiritual damage that these girls have is atrocious. The have been robbed of any childhood they might have had, and you can see it in their eyes—a vacant hopeless stare of someone who cannot see tomorrow.

When I learned what was happening here in Oklahoma, practically in our own back yards, I was led to do whatever I could to help these kids. Please keep in mind – this is happening only a few miles from Pryor, not in some third world country. Since last year when I sold my pizza store, I've been working on a new health and nutrition business, whose primary objective is to provide financial support for these rescued kids.

I sat down for dinner with Linda Caswell, she started a safe house for these kids in Oklahoma City about a year ago, and named her charity the All Things New Campaign. Linda has an amazing story about how she used to be a drug dealer, a prostitute, and involved with the mob in New Orleans, and how God pulled her out of that lifestyle and is now using her to rescue and rehabilitate victims of sex trafficking. Her organization takes in these young women and kids and puts them in a safe house where the traffickers cant find them. They are provided clothing, food, medical attention, counseling, and provided other basic necessities that we take for granted on a daily basis.

But most importantly Lindas charity is a Christian charity. I sincerely believe that after what these kids are put through, there's spiritual damage that can only be healed with the love of Jesus Christ. And no matter what kind of counseling or treatment they go through, if they don't have Jesus to cling to, I don't believe they can ever become one hundred percent whole again.

By adding in the header on the second page, it created some more eye relief, and also was its own mini headline, causing the reader to want to read further into the letter.

Once again, if you have numerous pages, and no headers to break up the text and pages it will begin looking like it's difficult to read. If I had to rewrite this letter again, I would have broken the paragraphs into still smaller ones for more eye relief, and added more headers.

 Use bullets. Bullets are themselves miniature headlines and create excitement in your letter. After your headline, they are usually the next thing you reader will see. Bullets should be filled with benefits to your reader.

Which brings up another important point. <u>Always</u> use benefits instead of features.
Your readers only want to know what's in it for them. I can't stress enough how important this is. This is probably the biggest and most common mistake that is made when writing letters and advertising in general.

Here are some examples of features

Fast delivery

Brand new ovens

Friendly staff

Great prices

Plug in delivery bags

These are all features. What do they say to your customer? Nothing really. You might as well tell them your delivery vehicle is blue and your staff wears red uniforms.

People are selfish! They don't care if you've been in business for 12 years. They don't care if you just bought new ovens. They really don't care if you just redid your logo with bright new colors.

If they can't see what's blatantly in it for them, then they don't care. Simply put, a feature is a color, size, price, etc.

A benefit will always tell your customer what they are going to get from the feature. Here's how we can change the above features to benefits.

Fast delivery: No more long waits! Your pizza will be at your front door faster then you can reheat yesterdays leftovers- plus- you won't miss a second of your favorite television show because you had to go pick up dinner!

Brand new ovens: Your pizza will come out of the oven piping hot with a golden brown crust baked to perfection in less than six minutes thanks to our new environmentally friendly ovens.

Friendly staff: Your order will be taken quickly and correctly the very first time you call because of our well trained staff.

Great prices: You can feed your whole family for less than one of those frozen chain store pizzas and still have money left over for dessert!

Plug in delivery bag: No more cold pizzas! Your pizzas will always arrive fresh and hot with that just out of the oven taste thanks to our electric hot bags.

See how the benefits quickly explain to the reader what's in it for them?

Now back to bullets.

Bullets quicken the readers pace and hit their hot buttons. Here are some examples of some great bullets.

- **You'll be getting over 30 different toppings to choose from!**
- **You'll have your pizza delivered in under 37 minutes!**
- **You'll be getting fresh vegetables cut daily!**

Always use odd numbers when listing your bullets, like 3, 5, 7 etc. Never list an even number of bullets.

On a side note, the number 7 is one of the most popular numbers for people. When asked to name a number between 1 and 10, the number 7 is picked more often then any other number. 1 and 10 are picked the least. 7 is a good choice to try using for the last number in your menu items. Example: **$9.97, $12.97, $15.97,** etc.

One of the first exercises that I'll usually do before writing a letter is sit down and list all the features. This will usually take a little bit of time, but once you're done, you should have a nice long list of features.

Then go about changing those features into benefits. This is an exercise that could take you quite a few hours if not a few days the first few times you do it. Don't give up, when you get it done, you'll have the basis for an extremely powerful sales letter.

The last thing to keep in mind when writing your letter is to keep it conversational. Don't get anal with it and think you have to spell every word correctly or have every sentence grammatically correct.

Actually… If it would piss off your English teacher if she read your letter, then you're right on track.

Being grammatically correct **kills** your letter. My wife has a minor in English. I would usually test a letter by letting her read it.

If she starts pointing out all my mistakes, I'm usually good to go with it. If she says it looks good, then it's time for me to start over.

By a conversational feel, I mean that the letter has to actually read like it's you talking to only one of your customers.

Use words like <u>you</u>, and <u>you will</u>, and hope to see <u>you</u> soon.

If you read your letter and it doesn't sound like your talking to someone sitting directly in front of you, you need to change it.

Don't use fancy words. Talk to your customer just like they talk. Use the word <u>get</u> instead of receive. "You'll <u>get</u> the biggest pizza in town!" sounds better than "You'll procure the biggest pizza in town!"

Use "transition" words to make your letter flow smoothly. Here are some great transition words.

"well, as a matter of fact"

"now naturally"

"and, of course"

Another great way to make your letter have a conversational feel is to ask a question, then answer it yourself.

Can you imagine that? I know it seems unbelievable but...

How do I get this great deal on this pizza? Its simple...

Do you understand what I'm saying? You do? Good...

When finished, here's what you need to do. Have an 8 year old read your letter out loud.

If an 8 year old keeps getting hung up, or stumbles on sentences, redo it until it flows. Your letter should be easy for an 8 year old to read without having trouble.

If an 8 year old can't read it, then most likely, most of your audience won't be able to read it either without getting confused or lost.

It's a fact that if you write over a 6 year olds reading level you'll start losing readers.

We'll begin the A.I.D.A. formula by getting their Attention.

This will be the headline of the letter. Most professional copywriters and marketers will say that the headline is 95% of the letter.

Some say its 100% of your letter because if the headline doesn't get your customers attention fast... and I do mean fast, then your letter has a good possibility of ending up in the trash.

Your Headline Should Be As Powerful And Direct As A Guided Missile!

Black Ops Pizza Marketing

Your headline <u>must</u> do two things.

The first you know is getting your customers attention, without that your dead in the water.

The second thing your headline must do is promise your reader something so wonderful – yet believable that they can't resist reading further into your letter.

Listen- people are extremely busy, you're only going to get 4 or 5 <u>seconds,</u> at the most to get their attention.

If you think a customer is going to read 3 or 4 paragraphs into your letter to see what you're offering them, then you've already lost.

So what kind of promises makes a powerful attention getting headline? Here's a few

- A powerful offer

- A FREE offer

- A limited time offer

Here's some examples of great headlines for your letter

FREE Pizza!

**FREE Breadsticks With Any
Large Pizza!**

FREE Delivery All This Month!

Always **bold** your headlines and make them larger then your text, and if they begin to get too long stack them so their more appealing to the eye.

The word **FREE** is an awesome word to use in your headlines. It immediately grabs attention.

Here's another way to tell if your headline is a good one. Ask the question "Who Cares?"

Here's a good example.

Melinda Jones Is Now In The Million Dollar Real Estate Club!

Who cares? Probably only Melinda Jones and a few of her friends.

Here's another.

Big Bobs Pizza Has Been In Business For Over 20 Years!

Once again... who cares? Probably just Big Bob.

Big Bobs Pizza Has Been In Business For Over 20 Years And To Celebrate Is Giving Everyone In Topeka FREE Pizza This Week Only!

Now who cares? Everyone who lives in Topeka cares.

Use this test every time you write a headline. If it doesn't pass the "who cares" test, you probably need to rethink your headline.

Ok, so we've gotten our reader to open our envelope by getting it into the A pile. We then grabbed their attention with our awesome headline.

Now we need to stoke their <u>I</u>nterest.

The best way to do this is to follow up on the headline that your headline proclaimed.

If our headline is **FREE Pizza!** The first paragraph should read something like the following.

"Its our anniversary all this month at Big Bobs pizza, and I'm wanting to give you a FREE pizza all this month! That's right, just pick out any large specialty pizza at menu price, and I'll throw in a medium one topping pizza, FREE!"

The first paragraph immediately told them again about the free pizza they could get. They didn't have to hunt through the letter to find the offer.

Now we need to get them to have a burning <u>D</u>esire to get our offer.

To do this we need to paint a vivid picture of what they're going to get.

This is where you want to use very descriptive words.

"Your vegetarian pizza will arrive hot and fresh with over a pound of freshly cut vegetables baked to perfection in a golden crust."

You have to use words that can actually make them taste their pizza before they even see it. Simply saying "your hot pizza will be there fast" won't cut it.

Now we're going to ask them to take <u>A</u>ction.

It's surprising how many advertisers will go through the trouble of getting a potential customers attention, creating an excellent offer, get them excited about the product...then not ask them to order.

It's like their scared or ashamed to ask for the sale.

Don't be afraid to ask for the sale. Tell them exactly what you want them to do. Be very specific.

"Look at the menu I sent you, pick out the pizza that gets your taste buds watering, then give me a call at <u>123-1234</u>. Your pizza will be on its way to your front door in minutes!"

See how specific that was. Tell them exactly what you want them to do.

You'll always end your letters with a P.S.

This should restate the offer and the guarantee. It's a fact that most people will read the headline of your letter first, then go all the way to the bottom of the letter and read the P.S. second.

Make sure your P.S. tells them exactly what they need to know even if they haven't read the letter yet.

"P.S. Please be sure to call and get your FREE medium one topping pizza tonight, but definitely before June 3rd

when this letter expires. And as always, if you're not satisfied, your money back, every penny!"

See how you can read the P.S. and know what the whole offer is? Always restate your offer, expiration date, and guarantee in the P.S.

Now I mentioned earlier that I would tell you about a "cheat" method to writing your sales letters. This is one of the easiest ways to write a letter, and almost every copywriter uses it.

What you need to do is "swipe" someone else's letter! Yep, find someone else's letter or advertisement that you know pulls a good response, and actually "swipe it."

Copywriters that write letters and ads for a living all have what's called a "swipe file." This file is filled with other successful ads and letters that they can go back to for ideas and inspiration.

Now don't copy someone else's letter word for word unless you have their permission, but you can use their letters as a template for your own. Make the letter layout and typeface the same as theirs.

Most copywriters will end up having hundreds of different letters and ads in their swipe file to pull ideas from. I suggest you do the same.

If you're still wanting to learn more about copywriting and go more in depth with it, Kamron Karingtons Black Book does an excellent job of explaining the writing process in detail.

On a side note. Kamron's Black Book Letter that's in his book is one of the best letters to use for the pizza industry. It's in my swipe file, and I highly recommend that you get a copy of the letter for yours.

When mailing out your letters, I recommend always sending a menu with it. Always have the letter folded so the headline is facing out, and the menu tucked behind it. That way the headline is the first thing the customer sees when they open your letter.

And never mail more than 2000 letters at one time. If you do a massive dump of 10,000 letters in one week, you'll be overwhelmed and unable to keep up with the business you receive.

Having this much business at one time, unless you're <u>really</u> prepared for it, will only cause you to give really bad customer service, resulting in pissing a lot of customers off.

<u>Grabbers</u>

Grabbers do exactly what they sound like they do, they grab peoples attention. I love using grabbers with my mailings.

Grabbers can be anything to make your envelope lumpy. This lumpiness invokes curiosity in the recipient. Have you ever received a letter or envelope that was lumpy and you could tell there was something inside it other than just a piece of paper?

Didn't you want to tear it open to see what was inside?

This is what grabbers do. They force your customer to open the envelope to see what's inside. Then once opened, they grab your customers attention so they will read your letter.

There's almost no limit on what you can use for a grabber. Use your imagination. The only catch is, you have to make it relevant to your letter.

You can't send out a letter with a deflated balloon attached to the top of the page just to get their attention and then never tie the balloon in with the rest of the letter or offer.

It's like someone running an ad in a magazine that says "SEX" at the top of the ad. But when you continue reading it says "now that we have your attention, here's a great way to clean your gutters with very little effort."

The headline might grab your attention, but as soon as you see that the rest of the ad isn't relevant to the headline, you feel like who ever ran that advertisement tricked you. Don't ever do this, make your headline or grabber relevant to the rest of the letter.

One of the best grabbers I've ever seen is a dollar bill. Yep, and actual real live one dollar bill attached to the top of a letter. I've used dollar bills as grabbers on some of my other business ventures outside of pizza on high ticket items over $100 per item to a highly targeted group of people with very good results.

I am just using this as an example though. I would not recommend using a dollar bill on your letters for pizza, unless of course your average order is over $80, which would be pretty incredible if yours is.

A substitute you could use for the dollar bill on your letters is a fake million dollar bill. You can get these dirt cheap for couple thousand of them, and several other marketers have reported that by using the fake million dollar bills instead of a headline, it almost doubled their response rate.

If you used the million dollar bill as a grabber, you could start your letter like this.

Dear neighbor,
As you can see, I have attached a crisp one million
dollar bill to this letter. Why have I done this?

Actually there are two reasons.

1. **This letter is very important and I needed some way to make sure it would catch your attention.**

2. **And secondly, since this letter is all about the money you can save this week only, I thought using a one million dollar bill as an eye catcher was a really good idea.**

See how we tied in the million dollar bill with the rest of the letter? Here's what the grabber looks like. You can find them on the web easy enough just by doing a quick search for <u>million dollar bill</u> or <u>one million dollar bill</u>.

You don't have to get too carried away with how you tie your grabber in with your letter. Just make sure that it's relevant in some way either to the offer or the problem you're solving for the customer.

Some other examples of grabbers could be attaching a string to the top of a letter. You could tell the customer that this string is to remind them that there's only a few days left to get a special that you're running.

And that by tying the string around their finger they will remember to order before it expires.

This grabber also works well if you have some charge accounts with organizations that are slow to pay you. Just sending them a bill may not get much of a response, but when you send the bill with a "magic string" attached, that you promise will remind them to put their payment in the mail if they tie it around their finger, you will probably get your payment faster.

For accounts that refuse to pay, you could attach a band aid to the top of a bill and tell them they're going to need it if they don't get you a check in the mail by the end of the day. (Just kidding, don't actually do that, you'll never get paid)

Here's a list of some other grabbers that you could possibly use.

- **Foreign currency**
- **Candy**
- **Band aids**
- **Aspirin**
- **Antacid packets** (these work great to attract attention about how your sauce wont upset your stomach like the other guys sauce will)

- **Rubber bands**
- **Bubble gum coins**
- **Small bags of your flour or spices**
- **Photos** (yes actual camera pictures or Polaroids)
- **Pennies**

Keep your eyes open for anything that you can get cheaply that might work for a grabber. Don't worry if you can't think of what you would use it for right away. If it's cheap and can be mailed, pick it up and store it until you come up with something to use it for.

One use for a grabber that I've seen that is absolutely brilliant was a message in a bottle. I never got to try this with pizza, but wish I had.

The National Academy of Sports Medicine does a lot of trade shows. One year they sent out to all the subscribers on their list a bottle. Yes, an actual clear plastic bottle. Inside was a map, printed on parchment paper that was rolled up and burned on the edges to look like a treasure map.

On one side of the paper was an invitation to come visit them at their booth at this years trade show. On the other side was a map showing the location of their booth in the trade show.

The bottle was mailed with a label and postage on it so you could see the map inside. How could you not pay attention to something like this arriving in your mailbox?

The result? A 75% increase in traffic compared to previous years trade shows.

Folks…this is the kind of stuff you need to be testing and using to skyrocket your sales.

If you wanted to try out the message in a bottle tactic on a small number of your customers, you can find the bottles at www.lumpymail.com. They also have numerous other grabbers that will get your creative juices flowing.

So if you're having a hard time coming up with a headline for your letters, try using a grabber instead.

<u>Voice Broadcasting</u>

So now you have a sales letter that's getting a nice response and is starting to build your customer base and bank account.

Now you're going to learn how to pull up to an additional 32% response from your letter by using voice broadcasting.

Voice broadcasting is basically where you send out a short recorded message to your customer. It only takes a few seconds to record and with the push of a button, the computer sends the message out to everyone in your customer list.

Now before you get nervous about using this, I want to assure you that you won't be using this tactic in an intrusive way.

We've all had one of those phone calls during dinner where you go to answer, and there's a politicians recorded message telling you to vote for him because he's the more honest of the two liars running for office.

<u>We're not going to do this</u>!

Not only will the way that you do this be nonintrusive to your customers, but you customers will actually love you for doing this for them!

Now there are a few rules to keep in mind when using voice broadcasting.

It can only go out to your customers that have done business with you within the past 12 to 18 months. You probably won't want to send it out to anyone who hasn't ordered from you any longer than that.

You cannot send this out to everyone in your community or delivery area. It must be only your current customers.

Laws vary from state to state, but at the time of this writing, there's absolutely nothing wrong with sending out a voice broadcast and contacting your customers by phone if you've done business with them within the past 12 to 18 months.

If you follow the directions in this book for doing this, you're going to be padding your bank account with the press of a button, and making your customers very happy.

The most profitable way that I have found to use voice broadcasting is in conjunction with a direct mail letter.

So you'll need to have your sales letter ready to mail out before you use this.

If your letter is going to go into the mail on Thursday so it gets into your customers mailboxes by Friday, you'll want to send out this message on Wednesday or Thursday.

All you have to do is call the company handling your voice broadcasting account and log in. You'll record a short message, and this is what you should say.

"Hi, this is Bob with Bobs Pizza, sorry I missed you. I was just calling to let you know that I dropped a letter in the mail for you today and was wanting to make sure that you knew to look for it. Talk to you later."

See what you've just done? By making the recording sound like you personally called them to let them know that you sent them a personal letter you're breaking down any sales resistance the customer might have.

You're not selling anything in this message. You're just calling them to let them know about something important coming in the mail. You're stoking your customers curiosity, so now they will be looking in the mail specifically for your letter!

Hell… You're practically their friend. After all, only friends call each other on the phone and send personal letters.

This tactic is extremely powerful. Remember, people like to do business with a person, not a company.

This is an extremely powerful psychological trigger. How many times do you get phone calls or messages from businesses that are trying to sell you something? All the time?

When a salesman jumps on the phone and starts spewing out his sales pitch, everyone immediately throws up their defenses. By not trying to sell anything, the customers defenses are not up, and now, they are going to be actually looking for your advertisement that's coming within the next few days.

Think for a moment how absolutely powerful this is. How many people do you know get up in the morning and can't wait for the mail to arrive so they can get the latest pizza hut flier? Not very many.

Now if both the pizza hut flier and your letter arrive in the mail on the same day, which do you think is going to get looked at, and which is going to go into the trash?

And the best news is… The big corporate chains won't use this simple tactic!

Now when you record your message, and have it sent out, you will be given several options.

One is to have the message played whenever someone picks up the phone. We don't want to use this option. Doing this would make this tactic intrusive.

The other option is to only have the message play if some kind of recorder or answering machine picks up. This is the option we want. This is very nonintrusive. The customer gets home from work, and there's your friendly message on their recorder.

If a real live person should pick up, the computer sending out the voice broadcast will simply hang up. The customer will only get dead air and will have no idea it was you.

What's the best times to send out your voice broadcast?

I usually would send it out twice. Once at 10:00am the second one at 2:00pm.

The first time I sent it out I would usually be able to leave the message with about 35% to 40% of my customer list.

The second attempt would only go out to the customers who I didn't get on the first attempt.

The second broadcast would pick up about another 20% for around a 55% to 60% success rate. The other numbers the computer hung up on because a live person picked up.

Now you might be tempted to just let the computer play the message to anyone that answers regardless of whether it's an answering machine or a live person so you get the message out to 100% of your customers.

Don't do this! You're shooting yourself in the foot and will have angry people calling you.

There are also other uses for voice broadcasting that can be very effective.

You could just leave a simple message like

"Hi this is Bob at Bobs Pizza, sorry I missed you. Just wanted to let you know that we're having a buy one get one free deal tonight only for our best customers. So just give me a call at 555-1234 to get yours delivered free of charge. Talk to you later"

Same basic principle, but no letter coming this time. Just always make the message sound like you were actually trying to get in contact with the customer personally to let them know about the special.

Don't overdo these messages! I wouldn't do more than one every two or three weeks. Even if you are coming off like one of their friends, everyone gets irritated, even with a friend that calls too much.

One final word about voice broadcasting. If you use this tactic as one of the main weapons in your arsenal, you will eventually have someone call to complain about it.

They'll call you up and tell you that your message was one of the biggest intrusions of privacy they've ever had in their entire life, and that you're a scumbag of the worst kind. Don't let one or two people stop you from doing something that's making you a profit.

Simply remove them from your call list and don't let it bother you. Some people live to complain about things. You know the kind of person I'm talking about. The person who complains about the 2liter that you gave them for free wasn't cold.

Or the person who complains because there weren't enough cheese pizzas in the mix of eight pizzas that you donated for free to a blood drive event. (ya, that actually happened).

As long as you're making money with voice broadcasting, you shouldn't stop using it.

24 Hour Toll Free Recorded Messages

24 hour toll free recorded messages are a very hot marketing tool to use to launch your business. Their extremely effective if used correctly, and extremely inexpensive.

And once again, the big boys won't use this type of marketing.

There are numerous ways to use the 24 hour free recorded message. I'll start by showing you how to use it in your local yellow pages.

Now the yellow pages is that dreaded black hole that sucks up every businesses advertising dollars and usually gives very little if anything in return. The funny thing is… Almost every business owner thinks they have to advertise in the yellow pages so their customers can find them.

I still have no idea why a pizza store owner would want their customers to look in the yellow pages to get their phone number, I mean gosh… that's the one place where every single one of your competitors are lurking, trying to snatch your customers away.

Now I could just make this tactic really short and tell you to save your advertising dollars and don't advertise in the yellow pages.

However since it seems so ingrained in business owners heads that they absolutely have to be in the yellow pages, I'll show you how to put an ad in the yellow pages that will make your competitors ads practically invisible, and cut your yellow pages advertising cost to a fraction of what they were.

Did I mention that you'll also be able to track the results of your yellow pages advertising now?

Oh, and don't let me forget to tell you my favorite thing about running this type of yellow pages ad.

It will absolutely piss off your competition!

This type of yellow pages ad is so effective that your yellow pages ad rep may refuse to run your ad. It's not that they're bad people and have it out for you.

It's just that it's in their best interest to have everyone advertising the same in their yellow pages books.

If one company starts pulling all the business, and the other businesses that advertise with them don't see a response anymore, then they have to deal with all your competitors when their ads stop working.

Think how many of your competitors actually depend on the yellow pages as their primary source of advertising.

Just think how mad they will be when they see that your ad is "locking down" their ad and drawing in all the traffic.

So as long as no one rocks the boat, the yellow pages ad rep gets to keep collecting exorbitant amounts to basically put everyones business card in the same place.

If your ad rep trys to talk you out of placing an ad like this. Don't let him. You're paying for the ad space, you should be able to put in that ad space what you want to, as long as it's nothing unethical.

Grab your yellow pages book and let's take a look at what's inside there right now under the pizza section.

There's not much that stands out here is there? Pretty much all the same. Name, logo, and phone number. Oh sure, some tried throwing in some extras like "we deliver" or something lame like that, but nothing that reaches out and grabs your attention.

Now let's look at what your ad should look like.

WARNING
Don't call any pizza restaurant until
you call this 24 hour free recorded message
1-800-123-1234

Does this ad have your curiosity, did it grab your attention? This type of ad can increase your yellow pages response rate by up to 300%!

By doing this, you've just moved yourself in the eyes of your customer from just another yellow page advertiser to consumer advocate, which is a very powerful position to be in.

So this is what your yellow pages ad needs to look like. It absolutely must stick out over all the other ads, and it will if you use this format.

So let's stop for a moment and think about what we've just done here by placing this ad over the usual yellow pages ad.

To begin with, we've captured everyones attention just as soon as they've turned to the page with our ad on it.

Then we played on their curiosity by telling them not to call any pizza place until they call this 24 hour toll free recorded message.

Next, we've reduced the size that our ad needs to be to grab attention dramatically.

Compare how much it will cost you to run an ad the size of a business card or smaller vs. running a full, half or quarter page ad with full color. You could be talking thousands of dollars depending on where you're located.

I've seen pricing for full page yellow pages ads on the east and west coast that could cost you well over 50k per year, and I bet most of the people placing these ads are not even tracking the results to see if their even making their investment back.

When using the warning ads, don't forget to include the three magic words – <u>free</u> <u>recorded</u> <u>message</u>. These three words are what will drive traffic to your phones.

Now the best thing about using a 24 hour free recorded message with your yellow pages advertising is that now you can track your results.

You'll know exactly how many people called your pizza store as a result of your yellow pages ad. This is a huge benefit over traditional yellow pages advertising.

Because you can add an almost unlimited number of extensions on your toll free number, you can include your toll free message number in different advertisements, and see which type of advertising medium is actually working for you.

It gets even better. You can also track how your recorded message is performing for you. Let's say that you record a 4 minute message. When you check your daily reports on your computer, you notice that a lot of people are hanging up at 3 minutes and 16 seconds into your message.

You can then go back into your message and see what it is your saying at that point that's causing people to hang up.

You can also switch messages instantly. Unlike a lot of print advertising, where once you run it, you have to stick with it even if it doesn't pull a response, you can quickly change your recorded message if it's not pulling the response you want it to.

So if this seems like a lot of work, or that it might be overwhelming, let me assure you that its one of the simplest and cheapest way to advertise.

Let's break it down into steps.

You'll set up your toll free number by going to www.itelecenter.com. They can have your new toll free number set up in just a few minutes and it will only cost you about $39 per month. You don't have to worry about paying for incoming calls, those are included in the $39.

Record your message by phone. This is the easiest, however, if you have a mic and can record your message onto your computer and save it, you can upload it at the website if you want.

Place your yellow pages ad using the "Warning" technique.

That's it.

Like I mentioned earlier, by adding different extensions to the number on the website, then having your customer dialing that extension when they call in, you can track which advertisement is pulling the best.

So let's say that you have your toll free number on your business card, in your yellow pages ad, and in two different newspapers.

One ad could have extension 1000, another extension 2000, another 3000, etc.

You can log into your account and see that extension 3000 had 75 people call your toll free number, while extension 1000 only had 9.

This would tell you right away that you might want to consider not advertising in whatever medium you're using extension 1000 in.

There's almost an unlimited number of ways to use your toll free recorded message with the "Warning" ads.

Use it on your business cards, on the sides of your delivery vehicles, in newspapers. While I've never used the toll free number with the warning message on door hangers, that could be a viable option and would be something to test.

Now you're probably wondering what kind of message you should use, and how long it should be.

As far as length goes, it doesn't really matter. As long as your message is interesting, you can go as long as you need to. I've heard arguments of both sides of this issue.

One side saying that shorter messages are better, the other saying longer messages are better. Most of my messages are under three minutes. But if you have a way to keep the message interesting, you can make yours longer. Once again, something to test and see what works best for you.

When working on your actual message, I've found it best to give the customer some information about something they didn't know about. Educate them. You don't want to just blatantly make a sales pitch when they call.
Here's an example of one you could use.

"Hi, this is Bob at Big Bobs Pizza. Did you know that most pizza stores allow their delivery drivers to smoke while they're delivering your pizza. Yep, by the time your pizza arrives at your door, there's enough toxins in it to make your kids sick. Now while the health department may not have any regulations in place yet to prevent this, I'm taking matters in my own hands and making sure that none of the drivers for Big Bobs Pizza smoke in their delivery vehicles....."

Do you kind of see what kind of message you should be putting on your recording? Your message needs to be informative to the customer, almost newsy.

And whatever you do, **never** bad mouth your competition. People can see right through this and see what you're trying to do. What would you think if you heard a message like the following.

"Hi, this is Bob at Big Bobs Pizza. Did you know that Ernie, down the street that owns Ernies Pizza uses cat piss in his sauce? Yep, and he rarely ever showers, and I heard his wife is a prostitute...."

Sorry, but Big Bob just shot himself in the butt. Never, Never, Never, badmouth your competition, you're the only one who comes out looking bad.

Now in the first message that Bob recorded, he never mentioned that his competitors allowed their delivery drivers to smoke while making deliveries. He just said that most pizza stores allow their drivers to smoke on deliveries.

If the customer that's listening to the recording automatically thinks that Bobs competition allows their drivers to get away with this, it's not Bobs doing. After all, Bobs just doing a little community service and letting people know what to watch for.

Record your message in your normal voice with your own personality. Don't try to be someone you're not and use some goofy "radio announcer" voice. It will come off fake sounding and hinder your results.

Just talk as if you're talking to one of your customers that's standing right in front of you. The message doesn't have to be perfect, it just has to be real.

I have been asked why not run the "warning" ads, then give your actual store phone number.

First, when your employees answer the phone, your customers are going to want to know why you placed an ad like that prompting them to call you, thus causing your employees to spend more time with them on the phone.

Second, you will have some people that call the 1-800 number that will listen to your message, and still not want to order from you. Unfortunately, there are some people out there who will never do business with you, for whatever reason they have in their brains.

There's no point in wasting time and money on these people. Just let the recorded message filter them out, and go about selling to the people who will buy from you.

At the end of your message, you can give your customers an option to leave a message for you, or press a number and be connected directly to your store.

There's not much of a reason to have your 1-800 number set up to receive voice messages, unless you're wanting people to leave comments or testimonials. And this is a great way to gather testimonials.

Be sure to look in the testimonial section of this book to see how to use these recorded testimonials.

Free Pizza Letters

This tactic is going to be used to grow your customer base. I used this for years in my pizza stores and still use it today in different aspects depending on what business venture I'm in at the time.

Most pizza restaurant owners will spend tons of advertising and marketing dollars to get someone to buy just once. Most of the time, if you factor in your advertising costs to get that customer in the door that first time, you're not making any money off of them.

This strategy is so effective, that I consistently had <u>at least</u> 100 new customers added to my data base every month.

Now not all of them became regular customers, but a lot of them did. And the ones that did become regulars ordered a lot of pizza from me.

This tactic works off the psychological trigger of reciprocity. This is a very powerful trigger, and by using it you're going to be adding new paying customers by leaps and bounds.

Once again… The big chain stores won't use this tactic. Oh sure, they might make some lame attempt by setting up a table somewhere and handing out some free slices, but that's about it.

Remember the rule- **we don't do anything unless we can track it**. We have to keep this rule in place.

If we set up a stand or table and just hand out free slices of pizza, we have to ask, how many free slices did we give away? How many of those people bought again? How many of those people bought after that? And how many of those people continued to buy and become regular customers?

You can't answer those questions.

Oh sure, you could probably add up the slices and figure that you gave away free pizza to 40 people. But you would have no clue how many customers, if any, you actually gained by doing this.

And how personal is it really to have someone standing behind a table handing out free samples? Is the person sampling the pizza really going to strike up some kind of emotional bond with the person handing out the slices?

Not unless the person behind the table and the person receiving the sample are a 16 year old boy and girl that think each other is cute and being flirtatious.

And I don't see where that's going to put very much cash in your bank account in the near future.

No, what we're going to do is going to be much more effective. What we're going to do is create an emotional bond with the customer and create a much higher return on the free sample you gave out.

The law of reciprocity is a powerful one. Have you ever received a gift from someone that you weren't expecting to receive one from? How did it make you feel?

Did you feel like you owed them something now?

That's how most people feel when they receive an unexpected gift from someone.

Now this powerful trigger can be used in an ethical way, or on unethical way. We're going to stay ethical with it.

Here's a great story about how some people use this tactic in an unethical way.

Back in the 1980s, Robert Cialdini, who wrote the book Influence: The psychology of persuasion, did some research at some of the airports.

He noticed that the Hare Krishnas would set up camp inside these airports and ask for donations. Now if they just stood there and asked for a donation, they probably wouldn't get very many.

But here is what they would do

They had these little goofy plastic flowers with them. When people would walk by them, they would go up to that person and pin one of the plastic flowers onto their collar or blouse.

Now the people receiving the plastic flower obviously didn't want it. They would say no thank you, or no I don't need that. But the Hare Krishna would insist and say "please take this, it's our gift to you", or "we want you to have this."

109

So the Hare Krishna would pin this goofy plastic flower onto the passenger, and then there would be this uncomfortable moment for the person because someone had just pinned a plastic flower onto their collar that they didn't even want.

At this point, the Hare Krishna would take a step back, smile, and ask for a donation.

What Mr. Cialdini found in his observing this was that it was easier for the passenger to give the Hare Krishna person a few dollars than it was to give the flower back and tell them they didn't want it.

Then after giving the donation, the passenger would continue on their way, and once out of sight of the Hare Krishna, would throw the plastic flower into the trash can.

A few minutes later, the Hare Krishna would get the plastic flowers out of the trash and start the process all over again with another group of passengers.

Whenever you give something away for free, it creates reciprocity. However the way the Hare Krishnas used it was in my opinion unethical and manipulative.

Now here's an example of how nonprofits are using reciprocity to get more donations.

Ever get those donation requesting envelopes in the mail from organizations like the Red Cross, St. Judes, or the Disabled American Veterans? Sure, we all do. Well check this out.

These groups usually could only expect about a one percent response rate on their mailings asking for donations.

However, they found that when they include those goofy free return address labels with your name and address printed on them as their "gift" to you, their response rate tripled!

This is the result of reciprocity. These people received something for free (even though they didn't ask for it) and felt the desire to repay these nonprofit groups for their generosity.

This is how we're going pack our customer base with brand new emotionally charged customers!

The first thing you to do when using this strategy is get a list of people in your area that have not ordered from you.

There's two ways to do this. The easiest is to get a mailing list from a mailing broker. Melissa Data has very inexpensive lists if you're just getting names and addresses. Their website is www.melissadata.com.

You're not going to be mass mailing these for obvious reasons. You'll probably have a mutiny on your hands from your staff if they have to handle the volume from 10,000 free pizzas being handed out.

I would usually shoot for mailing out about 10 to 20 free pizza letters per day.

The idea is to provide awesome service for these people since they have never ordered before. If they're having to wait an hour for a pick up, why would they come back and actually pay money for crappy service.

I would just start at the top of the list that your list broker sent you and check the address to see if it's already in your computer. If it is, don't send them a letter.

If the address isn't in your data base, just handwrite the envelope out right there on the spot.

There are some exceptions to this. If I'm going through my addresses, and I notice someone hasn't ordered in several years, I'll send them out a letter even if they're in my data base.

This will either reactivate the customer, or because we're using a first class stamp, if the customer has moved or no longer lives there the letter will come back undeliverable and you'll know to take that customer out of your data base.

The other way is to physically drive the neighborhoods and write down the addresses. I don't recommend getting your addresses this way unless you live in a very tiny town and have a lot of time on your hands.

But it's still the same principle. Get the addresses, cross reference them in your data base, and mail to the ones that are not in there.

One thing to keep in mind. There are some neighborhoods that you will not want to mail to. I know this is a dirty word in this day and age, but you will need to "stereo type" certain neighborhoods.

There's a government housing apartment complex in one of the neighborhoods in my town, I would never mail out free pizza letters to that area. And I'll give you three reasons why.

First: I would lose money. Second: I would lose money. And Third: I would lose money.

The people living there do not have money, they do not have cars, they do not have jobs.

Almost everything they have or will receive is from the government and is free. By sending them a letter for a free pizza, they don't recognize it as a gift, it's just another freebee that they may be entitled to.

You can test this if you like, but I promise you that if you send out 100 letters to that neighborhood, you would receive 95 of them back, and have less than 5 of them order a second time and pay for the order.

These are not the kind of people that I want to attract as my regular customers.

I do get orders from this apartment complex and we do treat them as well as we do any of our other customers. But we do get more complaints from these apartments as well. My delivery took over 30 min, I should get a discount. The driver didn't have enough parmesan cheese with them, I should get a discount (13 packets isn't enough?). My 2liter isn't cold enough, I shouldn't have to pay for it.

And this one is the real kicker...

I did send out letters to this apartment... once... never again.

Customer: I got this letter for a free pizza up to a $20 value and I want to use it.

Me: Great, what can I get for you.

Customer: Well, since its good for a free pizza up to a $20 value, I want to use it to get the special you have running of three large single topping pizzas for $19.99.

Me: Oh, I'm sorry sir, the letter is good for only one pizza, but you can pile as many toppings on it as you like up to $20 and I'll even have it delivered for free.

Customer: You mean I can't get the three large pizzas for free with this letter?

Me: No sir, I'm sorry.

Customer: That's a f#$%ing rip off.   Click

You know your neighborhood and market better than anyone else. So you would know better than anyone if there's a place that you shouldn't mail offers to.

When mailing these letters out, we will be using the same procedure we've done before. Hand written addresses, signature hand signed in blue ink, and a first class stamp.

I always put a dollar limit on the free pizza to keep someone from getting too crazy with the toppings. But other than that, there are no other restrictions.
Now you would think that if you mailed out 200 of these a month, you would get 200 people to respond for a free pizza with no strings attached. However that's not usually the case.

I've tracked this, and usually the most I've ever received back is a 61% response rate. Sometimes it's been as low as a 33% depending on the month and what area of town I was mailing to.

I always put an expiration date on the letter having it expire ten days after the date the letter was mailed. There's no reason you couldn't bump this up to 14 or even 21 days, but I wouldn't recommend stretching it out further than that.

The idea is to get the person to redeem it quickly so you can get them into your data base as soon as possible. And the longer the expiration date, the more likely they are to forget about it.

And of course, if someone calls in and asks if they can use it after it's expired, you can always tell them that you'll make an exception just for them.

Another important point. You absolutely must make sure that your staff is getting names addresses and phone numbers of the customers redeeming these free pizza letters.

If they're not capturing that information, you might as well have thrown cash out the window. Threaten them with the wrath of doom if you have to, but make sure that they get this information every time.

Once the customers information is in your data base, you will be able to mail to them on a regular basis with targeted mailings.

Now let's look at what kind of return you might be able to make using this strategy.

To make the numbers easy, let's say that you mail out 200 free pizza letters per month to people who are not currently customers.

Out of these 200 people let's say half of them redeem their free letters, that gives us 100 people.

The letters cost us .64 each to mail for a total of $128.00. We'll say the food cost on the 100 free pizzas is 3.00 each. This might be high, but let's say the customers pile on the toppings and max out the dollar value of the letter.

$128 letter cost + $300 food cost = $428

If only five of those customers become regular customers and order twice a month at an average order of $18.00 per order you're looking at a return of $180 per month which comes to $2160 per year return on your $428 investment.

And that's only for one month converting only 5 people to regular customers. You should definitely be able to convert more than 5 people per month if you're running a tight ship and doing things right.

On the next page is the actual letter I mailed out for the free pizzas.

Please – Let me treat YOU to one of my great tasting Pizzas – FREE!

Dear neighbor,

Hi, my name is Paul, I'm the owner of the Simple Simons Pizza right here in Pryor, and I wanted to make sure you've had the opportunity to try one of my delicious pizzas absolutely **FREE!**

That's right – **FREE!**

You can get one **FREE** pizza of YOUR choice – up to a $20.00 value!

Unlike the big chain stores, I don't have deep pockets to constantly run television commercials with the coolest movie stars talking about my pizza, or have those expensive radio adds constantly running between songs. I just have the best pizza in Pryor – and I'm willing to give you one for **FREE** just to prove it.

Look thru the menu I sent you, and pick out the pizza that gets your taste buds watering. Give us a call – let us know you have this letter, and YOUR **FREE** Pizza will be in the oven in a matter of minutes. Heck – I'll even deliver it for **FREE** so you don't have to come pick it up yourself – that's how confidant I am that we have the best pizza in Pryor and that you and your family will be coming back for more.

Please – call us at **825-5500** and YOUR **FREE** Pizza will be on its way, piping hot and ready to enjoy. Or – if you prefer to pick it up yourself, we're located right across the street from Wal Mart.

Hope to see you soon,

Paul Baker

P.S. Please take me up on this **FREE** offer tonight, but definitely before this letter expires.

This letter expires on **04/18/09**

Don't forget to use an expiration date to get people to redeem them faster.

Lazy Customers

Lazy customer is the term used for customers who haven't ordered in 30, 60 or 90 days.

Your lazy customer program is the safety net that will catch any customers that may potentially be leaving your herd.

There are two ways that you can try to reactivate a lazy customer. The first is to use the 30, 60, 90 day program.

Basically what will happen is at 30 days, you'll send out a reminder to the customer with some low priced free item to get them to come back in. I would usually do the free breadstick offer.

At 60 days, if the customer still hasn't ordered, I would up the offer, and give them a free calizone, which was a nine dollar value, or a free breadstick and 2liter for ordering.

At 90 days, I would send them a letter for a free large pizza in a last desperate attempt to keep them in my herd of active customers. When they hit this 90 day mark, you need to be concerned.

Some customers might have moved off. Some might have lost their jobs. Still others might have been swayed by a coupon from your competitor for a cheap pizza deal.

Whatever the reason, you have to try to get them back.

When the customers that hit the 90 days would come in to redeem their free pizza letter that I sent them, I would make sure that my staff or myself would ask them why they hadn't ordered in so long.

This is key, because you need to know what the reason is behind their long delay in ordering. If a lot of the 90 day customers started telling you that one of your staff members didn't make them feel welcome, then there's a problem that needs to be resolved.

I found that most of the time, the customer won't tell you that their buying from one of your competitors unless something happened that made them mad and resulted in them not coming back.

I know that one time, a lady named Linda redeemed her free pizza, and when asked about why she hadn't been back in so long, she straight up told us that her deliveries were taking over 50 minutes the last three times she had ordered, and didn't want to have to keep waiting that long.

Her telling us this, was worth every penny it cost me to give her that free pizza.

When we reviewed our drivers delivery times for the past month, we noticed that two of our drivers were taking almost 13 minutes longer per delivery than all the other drivers, and these were not new delivery drivers.

Black Ops Pizza Marketing

This was a problem that we quickly fixed.

So we have the 30, 60, 90 day program. The other way we can catch lazy customers is to just use a 45 and 90 day program.

After using the 30, 60, 90 day program for almost four years, I found that just by using the 45 and 90 day program, you would still keep and reactivate the same number of customers, and it was a lot less work.

The offer at 45 days was the same offer I used at 60 days, and I still had about the same number of customers hit the 90 day mark. So I would recommend just doing the 45 and 90 day unless you test it, and find your market to respond better to the 30, 60, 90 day program.

So after you decide which program you're going to use, then you need to decide on what you're going to send them. Postcards or letters.

I used the postcards for several years because they were cheaper to mail. At the time, postage to mail a postcard was .27 each, and the postcard cost me .17 each, for a total of .44 per customer.

The postcards pulled me in a response rate of 10.66%. Not too shabby of a response rate.

However, when I wrote a personal letter to these same people, my response rate jumped to 21.95%! That's more than a double the response that the postcards got!

Now it did cost me .50 to mail out a letter, vs. the .44 to mail out the postcard, but the difference in the response rate certainly made it more profitable to mail out the letter.

Once again, letters are much more personal than a postcard. I would recommend testing both in your market, but I'm almost positive the personal letter will out produce the postcard every time.

On the next page is a copy of the actual letter that I would send to my 45 day lazy customers. Once you have your letter written and saved in your computer, it doesn't take any time to print them out as you need them and sign them in blue ink.

Black Ops Pizza Marketing

This FREE calizone is for YOU!

Dear neighbor,

Hi, my name is Paul, I'm the owner of the Simple Simon Pizza right here in Pryor.

A few days ago I was looking thru my list of customers and noticed that you haven't called us in a while. So to entice you back, I want to give you a **FREE** calizone!

That's right – I'll give you a **FREE** calizone when you buy any large pizza at menu price, and I'll even deliver it – **FREE!**

I know how hectic things can get around this time of year – so why spend all that time cooking and cleaning when you can treat your family to a **FREE** calizone, stuffed with over half a pound of meats and cheeses and cooked to a golden brown.

You'll get enough food to feed your entire family – and for a lot less than you would have spent for just one pizza at those big corporate pizza stores.

Plus – I always put my neck on the line with every order – If you should ever be disappointed – for any reason, please let me know. <u>If I cant make it right – I'll give you your money back – every penny!</u>

Give us a call now! You'll get fast **FREE** delivery right to your front door, or you can pick up. You'll find us at 125 Steve Berry Blvd, right across the street from Wal Mart. Our phone number is **825-5500**

Hope to see you again soon,

Paul Baker

P.S. Please – take me up on this offer tonight! But definitely before this letter expires. The **FREE** calizone and **FREE** delivery are yours – and as always – if you're not 100% satisfied, your money back – every penny!

P.P.S. Be sure to sign up for our text coupons by texting the word **SSPPRYOR** to **74700.** You'll immediately receive a coupon for a **FREE** fountain drink –PLUS – a chance to win a **FREE** large pizza of your choice. You'll also receive coupons by text for **FREE** pizzas, **FREE** calizones, and **FREE** cheesesticks!

This letter expires on **06/11/09**

Notice how many times the word **FREE** is used, even though they are actually only getting one item for free.

The P.P.S at the bottom wasn't always on this letter. That's a reminder for the customer to sign up for our texting club. Once again, notice how many time **FREE** is used. There's more on the using texting in another section of this course.

Multi Sequence/Mucked Up Mailings

This is another tactic that will pull more money out of your letter mailings.

Most people will mail their letter once and that's it.

Now if the letter you mailed out just made you a decent profit, why not mail it out a second and third time?

Testing has shown that by remailing the same letter, or a slight variation of the first letter, you can almost double your results. What usually happens is that mailing numbers two and three combined will bring in the same amount of sales that the first mailing did.

So if you're first letter brings in $5000 in profit, letters two and three combined should bring in close to an additional $5000 in profit. This is doubling your profits just by remailing the same letter.

If your first mailing doesn't do very well, or doesn't make a profit, don't remail it. It will need to be changed or a different letter used. Only remail when the first letter works.

You can keep mailing after the third time if your letter is still pulling a good response and making you a profit. There's no need to stop dropping the bucket in the well if water keeps coming back up.

When you mail letters two and three, you might want to have the mailing house purge out the addresses that ordered from you the first time so you're not remailing to those names.

However, I have on several occasions just remailed out to my entire customer base the second and third time. No one ever complained about it, and we noticed a lot of the people that ordered from the first letter would order again with the second and third.

As long as the offer is making you a profit, I've never seen any real reason to purge the previous buyers out of the next mailings, unless you're trying to gather new customers by using steep discounts and have very little profit from the mailing.

I would usually try to have my second letter go out 21 days after I had mailed the first letter, and the third letter 21 days after the second. I always tried to make sure the follow up letters were mailed no more than 30 days after the prior ones were.

Any more than 30 days, and the customer may forget about the first one. And with this tactic, it helps if they remember the prior letter they received.

Don't worry about mailing too often to your customers. I've heard the excuse that if you mail too often then you'll make your customers mad.

This is certainly not the case. Research has shown that when you don't stay in contact with your customers, you can lose up to 10% of your customer base per month just by not staying in contact with them.

So if you have 5000 customers in your data base, and you don't contact them in any way for three consecutive months, you could have lost up to 500 customers in just that first month of not having any contact with them.

They simply forget you're there and drift off to one of your other competitors that is staying in touch with them by coupons or some other type of advertising.

Ok, so you mailed out your first letter and it received a really good response.

Now before we mail out the same letter the second time, we're going to "muck" it up.

This is a process where we can either use a computer software program like copy doodles, or you can simply use a red sharpie and muck up the copy yourself.

Copy doodles is an easy to use software that automatically puts handwritten words and markings on your letters. Their website is www.copydoodles.com. Check them out.

The other way to do this is the old fashioned way and just use a sharpie and physically put the markings and additional messages on the letter yourself. Don't worry about being neat.

The whole idea of this process is to make the letter look sloppy. Remember how we said good grammar kills a sales letter? This takes it a step further and makes the letter look sloppy. And the sloppier the letter is, the better the results usually are.

By jotting different messages, and circling different sentences on the letter, it gives it personality, making look even more like a personal note to someone and not something printed out in mass numbers.

On the next page is an example of a mucked up letter.

Don't Throw This Away!

You be the judge… if <u>Simple Simons Pizza</u> isn't the Best Pizza You've ever had, I'll give you your money back – every penny!

Plus--

Just for giving us a chance, I'll give you a
FREE Traditional Calizone
And <u>FREE Delivery</u> when you buy any Large Designer Pizza!

Dear neighbor,

Are you tired of greasy "fast-food" pizza? Are you disappointed with skimpy toppings? Are you frustrated by ninety minute (or longer) delivery times?

Finally – you and your family can get <u>Great Tasting Simple Simons Pizza</u> – **Delivered right to your home!** We're talking lip licking – eye-rolling flavor that'll blow your socks off!

Imagine, Savory Grilled Chicken, Roasted Garlic, Roasted Ham, and yes – Pepperoni for the kids. <u>It's blatantly high quality</u>. The flavor is rich. And, for those of you who indulge their family with the best – this is it.

No more cheap tasting pizza – <u>Now You Can Enjoy</u>…

- **Marinara Loaded with seasonings – not sugar!**
- **Dough made fresh daily with Olive Oil – not frozen dough disks!**
- **Fast FREE Delivery – not a $3.00 delivery charge!**

So, while everyone else dishes out that "budget" taste and screams for your money, my proposition is simple. Order a Large Designer Pizza – and I'll include a <u>Large Traditional Calizone</u> – **FREE.**

You'll get an awesome pizza, and a Calizone stuffed with over half a pound of meats and cheeses – *and* for less than you'd spend on a "mass produced" ordinary pizza.

But, the <u>VIP treatment</u> doesn't stop there – people who get the good stuff expect to be taken care of. When you order the best pizza in Pryor, its no different.

I put my neck on the line with every order – If you should ever be disappointed – for any reason, please let me know. <u>If I cant make it right – I'll give you your money back – every penny!</u>

Heck – I'm so confident that we have the best pizza in Pryor, that **I'll guarantee my competitions pizza!** If you decide to buy from any of our competitors here in Pryor, and are just not happy with the pizza you received, bring the uneaten portion to us, and I'll replace it with one of ours – For **FREE!**

Our top selling Pizzas are in the menu (a lot of people have gone crazy over the Bacon Chicken Ranch Pizza). Take your time, pick one out – then give us a call. Our phone number is **825-5500**

You'll get fast, **Free** delivery right to your front door – or you can pick up. You'll find us at 125 Steve Berry Blvd, right across the street from Wal Mart.

I hope to see you soon – sincerely,

Paul Baker

Better Hurry

P.S. Please – take us up on this offer tonight! But definitely before December 31st. The **Free** Calizone is yours – and as always – if your not 100% satisfied, your money back – every penny!

Don't get too crazy highlighting and circling everything. If you try calling attention to everything, you'll end up calling attention to nothing.

Now I'll show you how to use this tactic to create a three letter campaign that will absolutely pull in tons of sales into your business.

We'll start by getting pictures of your cheese. Yep, your actual cheese boxes, piled as high as you can get them. We're going to take a picture of these cheese boxes and use it as a grabber on our letter.

If you don't do a lot of business yet, and don't get in a large number of cases of cheese every week, just have your crew carefully save the empty boxes when they get done with them for a few weeks. Then stack the empty ones and the full one together to make what looks like one big stack of cheese.

Next we need to write a sales letter. This letter is going to be a "reason why" letter, and asking people for their help, two powerful psychological triggers.

This particular letter will be mailed out three times, and the second and third letter will be mucked up.

We're going to tell our customers that unfortunately, you really screwed up, and ordered the cheese this week, after you had already told your manager to order it earlier that week, resulting in double the amount of cheese you normally get.

This will give you a good reason to have a sale. I would prefer to give away something for free over using a deeply discounted price, but you could test either way and see which one works better for you.

Now staple the picture of all the cheese to the top of your letter. This will be your grabber, and will work as your headline for the letter.

Now after 14 days, we'll remail the exact same letter, with the exact same picture of all the cheese, the only difference is, we'll muck it up a little bit this time.

The first thing you need to muck up, is the picture of your cheese. Take a red sharpie, and either put a red "X" through about one third of the boxes of cheese, or mark a red line through several stacks.

Keep in mind that you will be needing to do this when taking the picture of your cheese boxes and adjust your photo accordingly so you can easily mark the boxes on it. You won't want a stack of cheese, and only a few boxes of it being in the picture.

After marking some of the cheese, write in your own handwriting with the red sharpie something like "**Only 58 boxes left!**"

Doing this will create some urgency in your letter.

You'll also want to muck up some other parts of the letter with your sharpie, and with a yellow highlighter.

Then two weeks after this letter goes out, you will send the third letter. You can either use the same letter again, or you can do a slight variation of it.

Take your picture that you already have of your cheese boxes, and mark another "X" through most of them, or cross them out with a line using your sharpie again. This time though, you want to mark through most of them so it only appears like you have a few boxes left.

Then in your own handwriting again mark something like **"Hurry, only 6 boxes left! When their gone, this promotion is over!"**

How well does this multiple, mucked up mailing work? How about an additional 3.7 million in sales for one business owner.

Bill Phillips who owned EAS Supplements ran an ad similar to the one I described to you. He wrote a sales letter advertising that he and his manager had both ordered truckloads of myoplex, a meal replacement powder, not knowing that the other person had ordered as well.

He had a picture taken of three semi trucks backed up to his docks, supposedly loaded with the myoplex powder, and attached it to his sales letter.

He mailed out the letter with the picture of the three trucks to his entire customer data base, advertising that he was discounting the myoplex 40% because he had over ordered and needed to get it moved out of his warehouse.

That first letter brought him in $4,000,000! Ya, that's four million dollars on one sales letter. Now granted his customer list was several hundred thousand people, but that's still a nice return on just one letter.

But it gets even better.

Bill remailed the same letter and picture two more times, each time "Xing" out one of the semi trucks to show that he was running out of the myoplex and the sale would soon be over. He also went through his letters and mucked them up slightly differently each mailing.

The result… The two other mailings combined brought him in an additional $3.7 million dollars in sales.

See how much money he would have left on the table had he not remailed that same letter two more times? Because your customer list is most likely not as large as his was, you probably won't unfortunately be looking at an additional few million in sales.

Still, your second and third mailing combined, should bring you in close to the same sales that you first mailing did.

On the next few pages is an example letter of what you could send out to your customers, mucking it up each time it's sent out.

Use this letter as a template to create your own multi sequence mucked up letter.

Dear neighbor,

As you can see I have attached a picture of a whole lotta cheese. Why have I done this? Theres actually two reasons really.

First, is I wanted you to see how badly I really screwed up last week.

And secondly, **I'm really needing your help with my screw up**, so I figured that the best way to catch your attention would be to attach a picture to the top of this letter.

You see, a few weeks ago I told my manager Catey that I would need her to place the cheese order for this week since I was scheduled to be out of town. My trip got canceled, and I didn't think anything about it when I went ahead and placed the cheese order like I normally do.

Well… Because Catey rarely ever forgets to do something that I ask her to do, she also ordered cheese, **resulting in twice the cheese I normally need for the next few weeks!**

I've got cheese boxes stuffed in every cooler and refrigerator I can find, so to make room I'm going to give you a **FREE** medium cheese pizza with the purchase of any large designer pizza.

Just look through the menu I sent you, pick out the large designer pizza that gets your taste buds watering, and I'll include a medium cheese pizza absolutely **FREE!**

Plus- I'll even deliver it for **FREE!** Or you can pick up if you like, we're located at 125 Steve Berry Blvd, right across the street from Wal-Mart. Our phone number is **825-5500**.

Hope to see you soon,

Pe Be

Paul Baker

P.S. Please- take me up on this offer tonight, but definitely before I use up the additional 75 cases of cheese I purchased, or when this letter expires on December 31st, whichever comes first. The **FREE** medium cheese pizza and **FREE** delivery are yours, and as always – If your not 100% satisfied, your money back – every penny!!

Here's the first copy of the letter that will go out. Be sure to staple or paperclip the picture of your cheese to the top of your letter.

Black Ops Pizza Marketing

2nd Notice!

Dear neighbor,

As you can see I have attached a picture of a whole lotta cheese. Why have I done this? Theres actually two reasons really.

First, is I wanted you to see how badly I really screwed up last week.

And secondly, **I'm really needing your help with my screw up**, so I figured that the best way to catch your attention would be to attach a picture to the top of this letter.

You see, a few weeks ago I told my manager Catey that I would need her to place the cheese order for this week since I was scheduled to be out of town. My trip got canceled, and I didn't think anything about it when I went ahead and placed the cheese order like I normally do.

Well… Because Catey rarely ever forgets to do something that I ask her to do, she also ordered cheese, **resulting in twice the cheese I normally need for the next few weeks!**

I've got cheese boxes stuffed in every cooler and refrigerator I can find, so to make room I'm going to give you a **FREE** medium cheese pizza with the purchase of any large designer pizza.

Just look through the menu I sent you, pick out the large designer pizza that gets your taste buds watering, and I'll include a medium cheese pizza absolutely **FREE!**

Plus- I'll even deliver it for **FREE!** Or you can pick up if you like, we're located at 125 Steve Berry Blvd, right across the street from Wal-Mart. Our phone number is **825-5500**.

Hope to see you soon,

Paul Baker

Paul Baker

P.S. Please- take me up on this offer tonight, but definitely before I use up the additional 75 cases of cheese I purchased, or when this letter expires on December 31st, whichever comes first. The **FREE** medium cheese pizza and **FREE** delivery are yours, and as always – If your not 100% satisfied, your money back – every penny!!

Only 36 cases left!

Here's an example of what your second mailing should look like. Don't forget to attach the picture again, and use a red sharpie or marker to "X" off some of the boxes of cheese. Don't worry about being neat, the sloppier the better.

Final Notice!

Dear neighbor,

As you can see I have attached a picture of a whole lotta cheese. Why have I done this? Theres actually two reasons really.

First, is I wanted you to see how badly I really screwed up last week.

And secondly, **I'm really needing your help with my screw up**, so I figured that the best way to catch your attention would be to attach a picture to the top of this letter.

You see, a few weeks ago I told my manager Catey that I would need her to place the cheese order for this week since I was scheduled to be out of town. My trip got canceled, and I didn't think anything about it when I went ahead and placed the cheese order like I normally do.

Well… Because Catey rarely ever forgets to do something that I ask her to do, she also ordered cheese, **resulting in twice the cheese I normally need for the next few weeks**!

I've got cheese boxes stuffed in every cooler and refrigerator I can find, so to make room I'm going to give you a **FREE** medium cheese pizza with the purchase of any large designer pizza.

Just look through the menu I sent you, pick out the large designer pizza that gets your taste buds watering, and I'll include a medium cheese pizza absolutely **FREE**!

Plus- I'll even deliver it for **FREE**! Or you can pick up if you like, we're located at 125 Steve Berry Blvd, right across the street from Wal-Mart. Our phone number is **825-5500**.

Hope to see you soon,

This offer will End Early!

Paul Baker

P.S. Please- take me up on this offer tonight, but definitely before I use up the additional 75 cases of cheese I purchased, or when this letter expires on December 31st, whichever comes first. The **FREE** medium cheese pizza and **FREE** delivery are yours, and as always – If your not 100% satisfied, your money back – every penny!!

Only 12 cases left!

135

And for the third letter, same procedure as the first two letters. Attach your picture and mark off almost all the boxes of cheese. Make it sloppy again, and let them know that the offer is about to expire.

If you prefer to use a headline instead of using the picture as a grabber, that's fine as well. However, having that picture in your customers hands does increase response to the letter.

This strategy came from a very unlikely source. In a previous section we discussed looking outside your industry for new marketing ideas, this one came from the credit collection companies of all places.

Credit collection companies discovered that a simple three step letter would collect what was owed to them over 40% of the time. That's really good results when you consider that they are not selling anything, and just collecting money from someone who hasn't paid their bill.

So marketing people figured that if it worked so well for people who were just collecting money and not selling anything, then it would probably work extremely well for someone who had a good product to sell to someone who wanted what they were selling.

They were right. Testing has shown that, depending on the product, most companies can make in the second two mailings, close to what they profited on the first mailing.

Just think how much money other businesses are losing out on because they just mail out one advertisement.

If you're profitable on your first mailing, you're leaving a lot of money laying on the table by not following it up with a second and third mailing.

Endorsed Mailings

Endorsed mailings are a type of "hybrid" between a personal sales letter and a testimonial. You probably know some other business owners in your trade area that might also keep a list of their customers.

These businesses might be dentists or doctors, lawyers, dry cleaners insurance offices or almost any other business that keeps a customer list.

Remember how we discussed that it can be up to 5 times more expensive to try to sell to a new customer than to someone already in our "herd" of customers? You do? Great!

Because what we're gonna do is borrow someone else's herd to sell to, and then integrate their customers into our herd. By using someone else's customer list, we're also going to cut the higher cost of acquiring those new customers.

Now there's several ways we can go about obtaining this other businesses list. First, if you're really close to the person and on really good terms, there's the possibility that they might give you their list of customers, or you could trade lists.

The other option is to make an agreement that you would give this business say, 10% of your profits for each customer that his list brought in, or maybe a dollar per sale that the mailing from their list generated.

Or you could just offer to purchase the list for a set price.

Obtaining the other businesses permission to mail to their customer list is only the beginning of this strategy. Next we have to write a sales letter that looks like it comes from the lists owner. And here's why we do this.

Look at your own customer list. These customers have done business with you, know you (and hopefully like you) and would more likely than not, trust your recommendations if you were to refer them to another business.

So let's say that you have a customer, we'll call her Sally. Sally eats at your restaurant several times a month, and is always recommending your restaurant to her friends. One day Sally is in your restaurant and mentions to you that her cold soda is making her tooth hurt.

She mentions that she know she needs to have a dentist look at it, but she just isn't sure who to call because she's terrified of going to the dentist because the last few times she went, it was really painful.

You tell her that you personally know a dentist named Tom who has an office right here in town. You tell her that Tom is one of the most gentle dentists you've ever been too and have never had a bad or painful experience.

Heck, you even trust Tom to work on your 5 year old daughters sensitive teeth, and it just so happens that you have Toms office number here handy, and that if Sally mentions to Tom that she knows you, Tom will do a free teeth whitening procedure for her when she goes in to have her tooth fixed.

Who do you think Sally is going to call to get her tooth worked on?

This is what we're doing with our endorsed mailings. The owner of the customer list is endorsing your business. You're essentially using his trust and credibility to bring new customers and revenue to your restaurant.

Now whenever you do an endorsed mailing, the letter must look like it's coming from the list owner, it can't look like it's being sent out from you. Also, you will need to write and mail the letter yourself.

You need to make this as easy and care free as possible for the lists owner. They might be reluctant to do an endorsed mailing for you if it looks like they are getting sucked into something that will put a lot of work on them.

On the next page is an example of what your endorsed letter should look like. Use this example as a template for creating your own endorsed mailing letter.

PICTURE

For my patients:

Why is your dentist writing to you about a restaurant?

Dear patient,

Every once in a while... and all too seldom... you get such exceptional service from someone that you just HAVE to "brag on them" to others. (I hope I deliver that same kind of service here at Tim's Dentistry.)

Last month I stopped into Agave's Mexican Restaurant, and I am still, frankly amazed at the QUALITY of service, and the authenticity of the food I received from Paul and his staff, who I had met at the local Chamber of Commerce a few months ago.

Paul had suggested that I come visit his restaurant on several occasions, but due to my busy schedule, I wasn't able to visit right away. If I had known at the time what I was missing out on, I would have rescheduled immediately and "made time" to enjoy the service his restaurant provides.

I had the Pollo Con Camaron which was a deeply marinated chicken breast grilled to perfection, then topped with spinach, cheese, and plump sautéed shrimp served over a pool of crème sauce. It was an absolute delight!

Anyway, I was so impressed with the food and service that Paul and his staff provided, that I decided to tell you about them. Of course, their not the only restaurant in town, you may have a friend or family member who owns a restaurant that you like to visit, and that's fine, but if not, I'd suggest you take my recommendation and give Agave's Mexican Restaurant a try. You won't be disappointed.

In fact, Paul told me that if you bring this letter with you when you visit, he would give your guests **FREE** chips and salsa, and another **FREE** appetizer of your choice just because your one of my patients.

Sincerely,

Tim Buchanan DDS

P.S. Be sure to use this letter by Oct. 31 when this offer expires, and be sure to bring the letter with you so Paul will know your one of my patients and you can get the **FREE** chips and salsa and the **FREE** appetizer of your choice.

Be sure to have the person (in this case a dentist) that's endorsing your restaurant sign the letter in blue ink before you have copies made. You'll also notice at the top of the letter there's a place to put a picture.

Here we want to put a picture of the dentist, or whomever the letter is from if possible. Tests have shown that by putting the picture at the top of the page of the person that wrote the letter, there is more believability and the response will be higher.

If you can't get the endorser to use their picture, that's ok. Just run the letter with a headline and your good to go.

<u>Postcards</u>

Postcards are cheap and easy to produce and mail. I always prefer letters over postcards though because in all of the testing that I have done, the personal letter has always outperformed the postcard for me.

Now this doesn't mean that there aren't certain tricks and strategies that we can't use the postcard for. This is one of my favorite tactics when using a postcard.

Most likely, in the past, you have received a postcard from a family member or friend when they are away on vacation. You'll get postcards from Disneyland, the Grand Canyon, Yosemite National Park, or some other vacation or tourist destination.

They usually have just a short message on the back of the postcard like "wish you were here," or "having lots of fun." The point being, you usually only get these kind of postcards from friends and family.

Now what if the next time you went on vacation, all of your customers received a postcard from you? Do you think that would make a positive impact on your sales?

Here's how to easily do this. Have your printer make you however many postcards you will need to send out to your customer base.

Have the picture on the front of the postcard represent wherever you're going to vacation at. If you're going to Egypt, have some pyramids on the front, or a camel. If you're going on a cruise, use a big ship. Just try to make the picture relevant to where you're planning on vacationing.

Then write on the front of the postcard "Even when I'm on vacation I'm thinking of you," or something similar to that. Then put a coupon on the back for whatever you want to give to the customer.

Bill Glazer who owns Gage Menswear, used this strategy by sending a postcard of him on a donkey in Greece. On the postcard was written "Who's the bigger ass?" It certainly grabbed attention, and was very hilarious, but be careful and know who your customers are. Grandma might not find it so funny.

Write the names and addresses on the back of the postcards and stamp them. Or, if you have your mailing house do this for you, be sure they will have them done before you leave.

You could just mail these the day before you leave, but to make this postcard more personal, you should mail them from wherever it is you're vacationing so the postcard will look like it's been mailed from the Disney land area, or from the cruise ship when it stops at a port in Alaska.

Just box up your postcards and take them with you. You can fit several thousand in a box the size of a shoebox, and your believability will be higher because of where they were mailed from.

Sometimes you might not be able to mail from your vacation destination. Obviously if you're going out of the country on a big game safari in South Africa, you would probably beat your postcards back to your home town by several weeks.

In this case you would have to mail them before you left.

By using this strategy, you're once again building a relationship with your customers that the big chains can't compete with, and it's very inexpensive. I purchased my postcards from color printing central. I could usually get 5000 full color postcards printed up for under $150. Their website is www.colorprintingcentral.com, or you can call them at 1-800-309-3291. Ask for Jenny.

Testimonials

Testimonials are one of the most underutilized tools that the independent owner has against the big boys. By capturing and using your customers testimonials, you're basically letting your customers sell for you.

You should be extremely grateful that you as a pizza store owner have this tactic to use in your marketing. In some states, chiropractors, and licensed financial advisors cannot use testimonials in their advertising!

So if John, your local chiropractor that does an awesome job fixing sore backs and shoulders, has one of his clients write him and say something like…

"John is the best chiropractor I've ever been to. I was in a car wreck a few years ago and have been living with back and neck pain ever since. After only three visits to John, I no longer have any pain whatsoever, and have taken up gymnastics because of my new found flexibility! Thanks to John, I'm better than new! You would be crazy not to go see John to eliminate any pains you might have!"

If you were suffering from back pain from a car wreck, and read this testimonial, wouldn't you want to give John a try? Unfortunately for John, some high and mighty politician decided that Johns business shouldn't be allowed to use testimonials in his advertising.

Fortunately for you, you don't have these restrictions. So if one of your customers writes you a letter saying...

"Big Bobs pizza is incredible! The pizzas I received we're loaded with more toppings than I was expecting. The nice girl that answered the phone, took my order quickly and was extremely polite, unlike some of the other places I've ordered from. Being a friday night, I figured we would have almost an hour wait, but the driver showed up in less than 25 minutes! You owe it to your family to give Big Bobs pizza a try!"

Wouldn't that testimonial have a powerful effect on anyone that read one of your advertisements with it?

Let's look at this scenario. You need to sell your home, and are beginning the unwelcome task of finding a real estate agent. The first agent you talk to tells you how great a job she does at selling houses. She tells you she's in the one million dollar club, and works really hard six, sometimes seven days a week.

The second agent you interview looks at your home, and takes some pictures like the first one did. However, unlike the first agent, she tells you "Choosing a real estate agent to sell your home is a really big deal, and you want to make sure you have the right person for the job, so instead of telling you how proficient I am at selling peoples homes, I'll let my other clients tell you what they think of my work."

And with that she pulls out a three ring binder packed full of customer testimonials from her previous clients. There's over 200 pages of happy customers joyfully praising this agent for how quickly she sold their house, and how much above market value she got for them.

Now which agent would you choose? The one that was blowing her own horn about how great she is, or the one who has over 200 people telling you how great she is?

This is what most pizza operators are missing in their advertising. Most will just scream about how they have the best pizza, or service, and most of the time it just falls on deaf ears.

However, when someone else screams about how great you are, people pay attention.

And the funny thing is… **it's so incredibly easy to get your customers to give you testimonials!**

Gathering Testimonials

There's a certain time in every transaction where the customer is the happiest about their purchase. In most businesses, this is right after the sale is complete.

Remember when you bought your last new car? How happy you were when the salesman dropped the keys in your hand? Or what about the last time you purchased your new big screen television?

With pizza, the happiest time probably isn't right after you hand them their pizza boxes, but it is right after they get their pizza home and take that first bite. This is when you need to get your testimonials, right when your customer is at their happiest about their decision to buy from you.

We don't want to call them in the middle of their meal and ask them to give us a testimonial, we've all had to take a phone call in the middle of dinner from a salesman, and it usually doesn't go very well.

No, what we're going to do is send out another short letter with their order asking them to give us a testimonial. And as a way of saying thank you, you're going to give them something for free when they turn in their testimonial.

Here's an example of what your letter should look like.

Black Ops Pizza Marketing

Dear neighbor,

From time to time I like to check in with my customers and see how we're doing. If you could take just a few minutes to fill out the testimonial form below, you would be doing me a huge favor. Plus, when you return this testimonial, I'll give you a **FREE** order of breadsticks just for taking the time to fill it out.

Thanks again,

Paul Baker

Name:_____

Address:_____

How many times have you ordered from us? _____

What is your overall feeling about my store? _____
_____

Please describe in detail a specific experience with us that you were happy with._____
_____
_____
_____

Please describe the one or two benefits that you have gotten from us that you value the most. Please explain specifically what you have gotten out of them._____
_____
_____
_____

Thank you very much, I really appreciate your honest answers.

___ **I do NOT mind if you use my name in any of your promotional materials.**

Signature:_____**Date:**_____

As always, I sign the letter in blue ink. This is reinforcing that they are doing business with a person, not a faceless company. I would only send out 10 of these every night, and not to the customers that have already completed one. Make sure that they give you permission to use their testimonial in your promotions.

One of the keys to creating your testimonial form is to structure the questions so you get the result you're looking for. If you simply put "please describe a specific experience with us that you recently had" you're likely to get some complaints about getting the wrong pizza, or slow delivery times.

While it is good that a customer lets you know about these complaints so you can fix them, we're actually fishing for positive testimonials on this form, so we need something that we can put in our advertisements.

By structuring your questions so you get a favorable answer, you'll have a lot of positive testimonials to use.

Politicians and political survey groups use this all the time. Ever get one of those stupid survey phone calls from your local honest politician that asks you some questions just so they can get an idea of how people really feel about an issue?

You'll have someone call up to poll you on a certain topic, like taxes. The survey taker will ask you a question like, "do you believe we should let little kids go hungry in school?" Well, most people because of the way the question is asked will automatically say "no." Who wants to let a little kid go hungry in school.

A few days later you hear on the news how 98% of the people in your community thought that we should allow the kids in school to get free snacks out of the school vending machines because they were getting hungry between classes.

Unfortunately, everyone in the community was going to have their property taxes raised to pay for the vending machines and all the free food the kids would be getting out of them.

Politicians unethically structure their questions all the time to get the answer they want. What we're doing is structuring the questions so we get the testimonial we want from a customer that has had a good experience with us, but probably wouldn't have shared the experience with anyone because no one had asked them about it.

So now that you have your testimonials lets cover what you need to do with them.

Testimonials should be used on every advertisement that you can put them on. I would even use testimonials on my take out menus. When I did use postcards, I would include a testimonial somewhere on the postcard. My letters usually had at least one testimonial somewhere on them.

One of the main points to remember, is that the big chain stores rarely, if ever use testimonials effectively. I always looked at their fliers that they sent out in the mail, and have never seen a quote from someone telling about how great they are.

The basic rule when putting out any advertisement in print, is to have at least one testimonial in that ad. The more you can get into the ad, the better.

In the other section of this book you learned about the free recorded messages. By setting up one of these 1-800 numbers, and asking your customers to call in and leave their testimonial, you can generate tons of great recorded testimonials for your store.

If you have any type of "on hold" system set up for in your store for customers to wait for their turn to talk to a person and place an order, this would be a perfect place to put these recorded testimonials.

Which would reinforce your decision to stay on the line while waiting, a message trying to up sell you before you have even gotten to place your order yet, or the happy voice of another customer telling you what great food and service they received?

Obviously the testimonial. If there's a long hold time, someone telling me about specials and up sells isn't going to get me to stay on the line very long. However, testimonial after testimonial will create the desire to stay on the line and see what all the excitement is about.

If everyone else is bragging on you about how good your food is, it's no wonder there's a long hold time, everyone wants to eat at your store!

Another reason to gather testimonials is because it reinforces the customers decision to do business with you. When they write down, on paper, what they like about you, it gets imbedded in their mind, it reinforces what they already think about your store.

Eventually what will happen if you continue to gather testimonials is you will create a following of raving fans.

These are the best customers to have, because they will sell your pizza for you.

One of the best things you can do after receiving a good testimonial from a customer, is to write a short thank you note back to that customer, thanking them for the positive words they wrote you, and letting them know that your staff was excited to hear about what a good job they were doing.

By doing this, you're promoting more positive behavior from this customer. When someone is thanked or rewarded for a behavior, they are much more likely to continue or repeat that behavior because of the reward.

These customers are much more likely to become one of your raving fans, and recommend you to their friends and family. Recommendations are the second easiest group of people to sell to. The easiest being people already in your customer data base.

When I do get a really good customer testimonial, I'll make a copy of it and post it where my crew can see it. Call me crazy, but it seems like the more positive testimonials that I shared with them, the better they performed.

If you think about it, your crew usually only hears about the complaints and problems. If that's all they ever hear about, then eventually they start thinking like that.

"All we ever do is screw up," "We can't do anything right." These negative thoughts constantly going through your teams heads will eventually cause them to think negatively, and doing so will definitely reduce everyones performance.

By constantly letting them see what they were doing right, it increased their performance, improved their attitude, and actually decreased turnover.

I highly recommend you share the testimonials you receive with your crew.

Texting

Texting is everywhere now and everyone uses it. I think to leave this tactic out of your arsenal would be a mistake.

Now to use texting in your store, you will have to have people "opt in" to receive your texts. The bad news is, this can be a slow process and could take a while to get people to sign up for your text club.

The good news is, that once their signed up, these are usually the best people to sell to in your customer list because they have raised their hand and said they want to receive offers and promotions from you.

While you may have a lot of phone numbers in your data base, don't be tempted to use these to text to. Texting messages and offers to customers who haven't given their permission for you to do so is illegal and will make some people mad.

Building up your texting data base is a lot like building your customer data base. It can be slow and not very profitable at first, but when you start getting a decent size texting herd, it will begin to make you money.

It took me two months to get my texting data base up to a decent size to where I was generating a decent profit. And lots of testing to see what offers pulled the best.

What's surprising is that you'll find out that the people who are in your text club will want completely different offers then the ones you put in your other ads and letters.

So how do you go about getting people to sign up for your text club? First, you put the offer to join out there on everything you send out. I used box toppers, table tents, and even put the sign up offer on my lazy customer letters.

The company I used was Sumotext. They had the users control panel on my computer set up to where every time someone signed up, they would get a return text with a coupon for a free fountain drink and a message thanking them for signing up.

Their control panel was extremely easy to use. You just download it on your home or business computer. You can then schedule your messages to go out on whichever day you want, and whatever time you want. So once you have your messages, dates and times programmed, you can almost forget about it, and it will do the rest of the work for you.

Just don't forget what days you have your messages programmed to go out. I forgot that I had scheduled a text to go out one day and didn't give my crew a heads up about it, and they got their butts kicked that night. I still remember the call I got from the girl answering the phones that night.

Employee: Did you send out a text tonight for $5 calizones?

Me: Oh ya, I forgot I had that scheduled on the computer to go out tonight.

Employee: Well… you had better get your butt up here pronto, because we have more tickets than the cooks can handle, and all the phones are going off at one time, and the line at the register keeps getting longer.

So don't forget what you have scheduled to go out and make sure you have staff in place for it. If you're interested in using sumotext for your business you can reach them at www.sumotext.com.

Did a few people sign up, get the free drink, then "opt out" of the texting club? Ya, but not very many. And the computer saved their phone numbers in the data base so they couldn't keep signing up continually get free drinks.

They also had it set up so every 25th person that signed up for the texting club would win a free large pizza. If someone won the pizza, they would be told they were a winner when they signed up, and they would get a free pizza coupon right there on the spot on their phone.

The words you use to advertise your texting club also have a big impact on how many people sign up for it.

Box toppers by far worked the best for me. But I found out that you can't just put on the box topper "sign up for our text club" or even "sign up for our text club and get a free fountain drink."

Nope, once again your box topper needs to be packed with benefits for the customer. They need to know what's in it for them. What they're going to get for signing up.

The first box topper I used was a basic black and white box topper with a picture of a pizza, a fountain drink, and our logo, with the words "sign up for our text club and get a free fountain drink." Ya, really exciting I know.

I put out 1000 of these box toppers and got a whopping 3 people to sign up.

When I decided to stop being lazy, I sat down at my computer and printed up a box topper that <u>told the customer what they were going to get</u> by signing up for our texting club.

Below is the actual box topper that I used.

FREE Fountain Drink!

Text the word **SSPPRYOR** to **74700** and we'll immediately send you a coupon by text for a **FREE** fountain drink!
PLUS
You could win a **FREE** large pizza of your choice!

You'll also be signed up to receive monthly specials that include **FREE** pizzas, **FREE** calizones, and **FREE** cheesesticks that are only available to our customers who have signed up for our text coupons!

Sign up now!
And get YOUR **FREE** fountain drink and your chance to win any of our large pizzas **FREE!**

Text the word **SSPPRYOR** to **74700** to get signed up today!

Notice once again how many times the word **FREE** is used. This really grabs attention.

After I started using this box topper, I averaged 80 signups every month. You can see that there are no logos and no color on this box topper, however it's very clear about what benefit the customer will receive by signing up.

The funny thing is, that after offering all those free things on the box toppers and in my other ads to get people to sign up for the texting club, no one really responded to free items being texted to them.

I would use the same free breadsticks, 2liter, and salad with any large designer pizza and only get a few people using the text coupon. Same thing with the free calizone or free medium pizza.

I really just kind of stumbled on the offer that really brought in the traffic. I would text out a coupon for medium one topping pizzas or calizones for only $5 each, pick up only, and the text coupon was only good for that night.

I got a decent response, but nothing great. Then I added this simple phrase and it was like turning on a water hose full blast. **Limit 5 per customer at this price**.

When I started texting out that sentence with the rest of the offer, my response almost doubled. The first time I used it, we had 338 people signed up to receive the texts. We sold 76 medium one topping pizzas within four hours after texting that.

And we had very few orders for just one pizza. Actually almost half of the people that ordered wanted five!

By simply putting a limit on how many pizzas someone could get, it caused people to look at the offer differently.

Instead of just being a $5 pizza deal, now it's such a great offer that they have to put limits on it or they might sell out. Of course if someone said they needed six or seven pizzas, we always said we could sneak a few extra ones over the limit in because the boss wasn't there that night to enforce the five per customer limit.

I would usually run the texts on a Monday or Tuesday night, which were the two slowest days of the week for us, usually having the texts go out sometime between 4pm and 5pm, so the message was fresh on peoples minds when they were getting ready to leave work and wondering what to do about dinner.

I did test sending out the text before lunch several times, however every time we did this, it reduced the overall response rate for the day. We would have a few people use the text coupon at lunch, but we found that most of the coupons redeemed came after 5pm.

People have so much going on throughout their day, that if you send them a text that early, they will usually forget about it by 5pm. By the time they remember it again, they are already home and didn't feel like getting out again.

Having the text sent out right before the majority of people get off work, would always work best for me. They could just stop by on their way home from work and pick up their pizzas.

This is something you will want to test for your market though. If a majority of your business comes from lunch sales, you may want to send your texts out right before lunch.

Test both ways and see which works best for you.

Thank You Bounce Back Card

This is a <u>very</u> inexpensive tactic that brings in great returns in a very short amount of time. The key to using this tactic is disciplining yourself to take the time to do it on a daily basis.

This strategy involves getting a box of thank you cards from your local drug store or retail store.

I got a generic thank you card at my local Wal-Mart for $5.87 for a box of 50 cards. I would usually buy several boxes at a time so I would have enough for a few weeks.

Next, you need to look at your point of sale system, or whatever other system you use to track your data, and see approximately how many deliveries that you have every day of the week.

So if you determine that you're going to have around 40 deliveries that night, then grab 40 thank you cards and a blue ink pen, and get ready to write.

Now open each card and in <u>blue ink</u>, and using your <u>own</u> <u>handwriting</u> write the following message…

Black Ops Pizza Marketing

Hi Bill,

I just wanted to personally thank you for your order tonight. I really appreciate it. Please use this card for a free order of bread sticks on your next order anytime within the next 30 days.

Thanks again,
Paul

Once again, use blue ink and your own handwriting.

The easiest way to prep these is to leave off the "Hi Bill" at the beginning of the card.

When an order is placed, just grab one of the pre written cards, and using the same color ink pen that you used to write the message.

Write in the customers name, throw the cards in one of the envelopes that came with the cards and write the customers name on the back of the envelope.

Here's where it gets tricky because you're depending on your delivery driver from here on out .

When your driver gets to the door and hands the customer their pizza, right after the driver has collected the money, the driver needs to say "Oh"… (In their best I almost forgot voice)

"Paul wanted me to give this to you"

The driver needs to say this using your name. Don't let them get away with saying nothing and just laying the card on top of the boxes when he hands them their pizza.

This is what makes this tactic work, and what makes the card look special in the eyes of the customer.

When your customer gets a card that is hand written, and personally signed by you, and your driver specifically says that you wanted them to have this card, you're making that customer feel extremely important.

I know that you're probably thinking that you're too busy to sit down and write out these cards, but let's take a look at the potential numbers and see how much money you might be leaving on the table.

When I did this strategy, I usually did send out 40 cards a day.

It did take me about a good 20-30 minutes per day to sit down and write out the cards.

Because most of the people I handed these out to were regular customers, I had an average return rate on these of 63%

This is an extremely high return rate and quite honestly it shocked me when I started checking my point of sale system to see how many were being turned in.

So on a weekly basis, I sent out around 280 cards, costing me roughly 41.00 in cards per week.

Within the next 30 days (because of the expiration date) I would have around 175 of these cards turned in.

A that time, my average order was about 18 bucks, and the cheese sticks cost me 1.19 to make.

Out of the $18.00, $5.40 went to food cost. So after doing the math, I had an average net profit of 11.41 per order.

$11.41 net profit x 175 thank you cards redeemed = $1996.75

When I subtract the cost of the cards, which was $41.00 from the $1996.75, I usually ended up with a net profit of **$1955.75**. And that's only one weeks worth of cards!

I did notice that the numbers seemed to start going down after about four months of constantly using this tactic. When the customers started getting multiples of these cards, they didn't look as personal and started losing their effectiveness.

At this point the card just became another "free breadsticks" coupon to them.

I would recommend using this tactic for a few months, then giving it a break for a few months so it doesn't lose its ability to generate cash quickly.

Using Disasters To Generate Cash

This strategy involves using any kind of disaster that might happen in your store to generate cash from your customers.

This tactic works best with your customer base, but could be used as a mass mailing to everyone in your area.

Have you ever had something bad happen? Something that really put a financial strain on you? Most all of us have at one time or another. Equipment breaking down, floods, accidents, etc.

By using this strategy, you're now going to be able to take these disasters and profit from them. I know this might sound like there's no way something like this would work, but once you know the psychology behind it, you'll understand why it can't fail.

When friends have a disaster in their life, what usually happens? Most of the time that persons friends will jump in to help them out. Overall, people are good natured and actually want to help out other people.

Look how much money is donated to other countries when those countries experience a natural disaster like a tsunami or hurricane. People want to jump in and help other people out. It's just human nature.

What we're going to do is ask your "friends" (everyone in your customer base) to help you out of a tough situation. You're going to tell them how something bad has just happened to you and that you need their help.

By doing this, not only are you using their natural desire to help a friend out, you're also making them feel like they have just been let inside your inner circle of friends.

It's that inner circle of friends that only a few are allowed to be inside. The friends that get to know most of what's going on in your life, even the bad stuff.

One of the best letters I ever mailed out was to 6300 people in my zip code. It basically told them that one of my Lincoln ovens had went out and the repair bill was going to cost me over $4000 (it really did, some stupid blower motor part went out)

Honestly, I think the repair guy screwed me on the cost because he knew I needed it fixed fast… but whatever.

This letter went out the first week in December. And it told everyone that I was short on funds because of the extremely high cost of the bill. I told them that I wasn't sure if I could come up with the money by the time it needed to be paid on the first of January, and might have to lay off some of my staff, or at the very least cut their hours to be able to come up with the money.

I told them that I really didn't want to have to do this to them this close to Christmas, but I've been financially backed into a corner and wasn't sure what else to do. I told them I could really use their help and offered a free breadstick and free 2liter in the letter with the purchase of a large specialty pizza.

The result was absolutely crazy. I did make enough to cover the repair plus a lot more. The most important thing though, was the fact that we had lots of people that when they called, were making sure that we knew they were helping us out.

Everyone loves to help someone else out of a tough situation, it makes them feel good about themselves.

I also used letters to ask for help with several other disasters that came along.

One time our refrigeration guy was moving our ice machine and forgot to tighten down a high pressure water hose. In the middle of the night, the hose popped off, and at 5:30 in the morning, I got a call from the shopping centers maintenance man telling me that I had water pouring out of the doors in my store. I arrived to find the store completely flooded.

Another time, we lost the lease on our building and had to move. When we got reopened, I sent out a letter reminding everyone what had happened and told them how the move had financially drained me.

I certainly didn't bring in nearly enough sales from that letter to pay for the move, but it did generate a nice profit.

Don't be afraid to tell people if you financially need help because something bad has happened, even if you really don't, tell them anyway, it once again puts a personal face on your business. And people like doing business with a person, not a company.

On the next page is the actual letter I used when my oven broke down. Use this letter as a template for the next time you have a disaster in your business and need to generate some quick cash.

You'll get the Best Pizza in Pryor!
<u>Plus.</u>
FREE Ice Cold 2 liter
FREE order of Garlic Cheese Sticks
FREE Delivery

Dear neighbor,
Hi my name is Paul and I own the Simple Simons Pizza right here in Pryor. We make delicious hand made pizza for carryout or **FREE** delivery.

I just got hit with a mind boggling oven repair bill. I didn't see it coming, and frankly – it's really put the squeeze on me. My repair guy tried to keep the bill as low as he could, but because it was one of the main parts in the oven, the bill came to $3998!

I'm trying to give my employees as many hours as possible this close to the christmas season, but with a repair bill this size, I'm going to have to make cuts somewhere. My backs against the wall – and I could really use your help.

So, for every large Designer Pizza you order this month, I'll throw in **FREE** Garlic Cheese Sticks, a **FREE** 2 liter of Pepsi – and I'll even deliver it for **FREE**! Plus... You can even use this letter as many times as you want until December 31st.

You can pick up, or take advantage of our **FREE** delivery. You'll find us at 911 S. Mill st. right next to Heartland Video. Our phone number is **825-5500**.

I appreciate your help.

Sincerely,

Paul Baker

P.S. Please take me up on this offer tonight, but definitely before January 7th, when my repair bill comes due. The **FREE** breadsticks and **FREE** Pepsi are yours – and as always – if your not 100% satisfied, your money back – every penny!

Be sure to put a short expiration date on your letters of usually two to three weeks so your letters have a sense of urgency about them.

Black Ops Pizza Marketing

FREE Pizza all Month!

Dear neighbor,

A few days before Christmas, my landlord came to visit me at my store. I assumed he was stopping by to talk about renewing our lease (we've been there over 15 years) – or to talk about some other small busines matter.

As we sat down, he got right to the point, and told us that they decided to lease our building out to a large company – and that we had 45 days to be out – no opportunity to match the other companys offer on the building or renegotiate the lease in any way.

A lot of things start going thru your head when you hear news like that – how do I find a new location in 45 days? How do I pay all the bills with no money coming in? And most importantly -- How do I tell my employees that they are about to be unemployed this close to Christmas?

After months of praying, and telling our unemployed crew – "just a few more weeks" – God has blessed u with a new location right across the street from Wal Mart.

I need your help...

...Before we found out the horrible news of loosing our lease – I had promised Christmas bonuses to my employees -- some of which were depending on that bonus to help buy presents for their kids. Now that we're reopened – I feel obligated to pay them the Christmas bonus they were expecting.

After three months of no income – and having to spend every penny of my life savings to get this store reopened -- I'm short on funds to give them their late Christmas bonuses. So, in return for your help, I'm giving away a **FREE** medium single topping pizza with the purchase of any large designer pizza. Plus – I'll even deliver it for **FREE*** or you can pick up. Our new location is at 125 Steve Berry Blvd. right across the street from Wal Mart. Our phone number is still **825-5500**.

As always – if my pizza doesn't live up to your expectations – if it's not what you expected in every way - just let me know – If I cant make it right – I'll give you your money back.

Hope to see you soon – sincerely,

Paul Baker

Paul Baker

P.S. Please – take me up on this offer tonight! But definitely before July 31st The **FREE** medium single topping pizza and **FREE** delivery are yours – and as always – If your not 100% satisfied, your money bacl – every penny!

Here's another letter I used when we lost our lease and had to move to a different location. I sent out 6500 of these letters and had 479 redeemed.

<u>Warning Label On Boxes</u>

Even though the warning ads and 24 hour toll free recorded messages have already been covered, I believe that this particular strategy that uses those techniques is so powerful and effective that it needed its own section.

This tactic will once again put a personal touch to the transaction, and further the "relationship" between the store owner and the customer.

You'll need to have a printer create this warning label on a sticker for you. I usually used a sticker that was 2 ¼ inches by 6 inches. I could usually get these printed up for about $350 for 5000 of them.

The sticker would read

WARNING!
Don't Open This Box Yet!
Before you even open this box, first call to hear a free recorded message from Paul at 1-800-123-1234. Paul has an important message for you to hear BEFORE you open this box.

I would have my staff put one of these stickers on every order that went out.

When the customer called the toll free number to see what was going on I would have a recorded message that I recorded myself that said the following.

"Hi, this is Paul. I just wanted to personally thank you for your order tonight, and wanted to let you know that it's because of you that my employees and myself have jobs and have food on the table for our families. Without you, none of us have what we do, and I just wanted to personally thank you for your patronage. Enjoy your meal and have a great night.

Wow… is that powerful or what?

How many times have you purchased something, from almost any business, and <u>never</u> received a thank you of any kind.

I dropped 44k for a sports car for my wife back in 2005. Once we had the car off the lot, we never heard from the dealer again. Think about that… making a purchase that large, and they don't follow up with just a simple thank you card.

Now your competition is probably having their staff give a half hearted "thank you, have a nice night" after a customer picks up their order, but I promise you, it has nowhere near the impact that this does.

By telling your customer that they're the reason you're able to feed your family and provide jobs for your employees, you just made their purchase personal.

They're not spending their money with a huge corporate conglomerate that's just depositing their funds into a never ending bank account.

They're spending their money with a real human being that really appreciates them.

As an added bonus, by using this, it will decrease the number of people calling to complain or get a refund.

If someone does have a problem or complaint, I've noticed that they are a lot nicer about it because of this message. After all, now they realize that their talking to a real person about their problem and not some big faceless corporation.

This tactic is **too easy** to not use to build a relationship with your customers. And with the toll free number only costing you $39 per month to do this, it's a no brainer.

<u>Your Guarantee</u>

Most pizza store owners don't look at their guarantee as a marketing tactic. They think it's just there in case someone gets pissed off and wants their money back.

You need to realize, that if you have a guarantee and are not promoting it, then you have all the liabilities that a guarantee brings and none of the benefits.

Look at it this way. You're probably an honest store owner. If someone honestly wasn't happy with their pizza, and wanted their money back, would you give it to them?

If you or your staff completely screwed up their order, and couldn't make it right, wouldn't you give them their money back if they asked for it?

What about in the worst case where you know the person is just being difficult and a pain in the butt. Wouldn't you just give them back their money so you wouldn't have to fight and argue with them?

If you would, then you have a guarantee, and only have the liabilities associated with one.

Now if you have a guarantee and you're posting it on every piece of advertising that comes out of your store, then you're getting the benefits that your guarantee provides.

Lots of business owners, not just pizza store owners, are scared to openly display their guarantee. They're afraid that if they publicly show their guarantee and display it, they will have tons of refunds and they might go out of business because everyone will want their money back.

There may be a few people who will try to take advantage of you offering a guarantee, but most people are honest.

I've mailed out personal letters with my guarantee on them for over six years, and out of over 100,000 letters mailed out over that time period, I gave out less than 12 refunds because someone said they didn't like the pizza and wanted their money back.

Oh sure, I did have to refund some money because of other problems that were legitimately our fault like slow delivery times or the drivers getting the orders switched around.

But the amount of money that you will have to refund is so small and tiny it's not worth worrying about or stressing over.

If you do begin getting a lot of requests for refunds, you might have deeper issues you need to get straightened out before you continue to advertise much more.

Another reason to proudly display your guarantee is to get the fence sitters over to your side.

By taking all the risk, the customer doesn't have to worry about getting screwed on a bad pizza.

Black Ops Pizza Marketing

Here's a good story to demonstrate what I mean.

A man wanted to buy a horse for his daughter. There were two horses for sale. The first man that he talked to told him "Buy the horse, take it home, I'll cut you a great deal on him at $750, and I'll even throw in a sack of oats to feed him with for the next few days."

The second man he talked to told him "My horse is kind, gentle and good, but I would say that, it's my horse. Tell you what… Let me bring the horse over to you. I'll let your daughter ride the horse for the next 30 days. I will even send my son over to your home every day to feed, water, and clean up the debris the horse leaves during this time. At the end of the 30 days, you decide if the horse is suitable for your daughter. If it is, I will ask to be paid for the horse. If it is not, I will come pick up the horse at my expense."

You may have already heard this story, but it shows how powerful a strong guarantee can be. There's no risk at all on the second horse.

Now other pizza places, especially the big chains are not willing to put a guarantee out there. They're like the guy with the first horse. This makes your store stand out even more because of this.

When all pizza stores are the same in an area, the one with the strongest guarantee wins!

The amount of business that promoting your guarantee will generate will by far outweigh the few people that do try to take advantage of you.

And don't just put something like "we guarantee our pizzas" out there.

Be specific. Make it iron clad. Make it attention getting.

Big Dave Ostrander created a guarantee that actually guaranteed his competitions pizza. He advertised that if you didn't like the pizza you got from one of his competitors, he would replace it with one of his for free! Now that's powerful.

Joe Polish is a marketer that taught carpet cleaners how to market their businesses. He would run a three day boot camp where these carpet cleaners would pay $10,000 each to come and learn how to market their business.

Joe would guarantee that if you didn't think the boot camp was everything that you expected, or didn't live up to everything that was promised, or for whatever reason you weren't happy with the boot camp, even after just the first day, he would give you back your money, plus an additional $500 to pay for your flight home.

Joe has had well over a thousand people go through his boot camps with this guarantee, and has never had anyone ask for their money back and the $500 bucks.

Now if you do make an outrageous guarantee (and you should) you must be able to live up to it. Don't make a 12 min delivery guarantee and wonder why you're refunding half your orders.

You're guarantee has to be something you can live up to.

Fundraising Letters

If your business is anything like mine was, then you probably almost need a calculator to keep track of how many different charities and organizations contact you looking for donations.

At first, I would usually give a little bit of money or donate pizza, depending on what the need was of the organization. Sometimes they just needed to feed a few kids from a local church who were mowing the lawns of the elderly people in town.

Sometimes, however, there was a need for actual money to be raised so kids could go to church camp, or on school trips. At first I would donate some free pizza coupons to be raffled off. This was a cheap and easy way for me to help the group out without letting go of my hard earned cash.

Then a youth pastor came in one day and asked if we could make any financial donations for the kids who couldn't afford to go to church camp. They had nine kids who wanted to go, but whose parents couldn't afford the $299 to send them for the week.

They only had three weeks to raise the money and had already had a small bake sale at their church, but were still extremely short of gathering all the money they needed.

So we came up with a plan that turned out to be a gold mine for both of us.

I wrote a quick sales letter that told how these kids were trying to raise money for church camp and were coming up really short. So to help them out, I would donate three dollars for every large pizza, and two dollars for every medium pizza that was sold at menu price when the customer brought in the letter, or mentioned they had the letter when they called in their order.

It took me less than 30 minutes to write the letter, and I printed off 11 copies of it for them to use, costing me a whopping 88 cents in paper cost.

For the next two weeks, the youth group made copies of the letter and handed them out to the community. I honestly have no idea how many copies they handed out, and they said they didn't keep track of how many they made.

But when the weekend came for those letters to be redeemed, we had 113 letters redeemed resulting in an additional $1287.32 in sales!

We started accepting the letters on a Friday, and ended it on that following Sunday night.

Now $1287 might not seem like a lot of extra money over three days, however, keep in mind that the investment to get this was only 88 cents, and 30 minutes of my time.

While you could just sit back and wait for organizations to contact you for donations, there is a better way.

By being proactive in your approach, you can actually turn what other people see as financial donating and community involvement into a steady stream of additional income.

The best way to use this strategy is to sit down and make a list of possible organizations that will be needing funds. Church and school groups are the two big ones, but there's also boy scouts, sports clubs, 4H clubs, and archery clubs. There's some kind of club for almost every aspect of life out there if you look for it… I even had a local raccoon hunters club in my town…who knew.

If you're going to promote this strategy, what you want are the organizations that have large memberships with a lot of young teenage people. Once again, church and school groups usually fit this profile the best.

You'll want to contact these organizations twice. First with a letter, then with a phone call.

Your letter doesn't need to be a sales letter, just a basic person to person letter explaining that you can help that organization raise a reasonable amount of funds for whatever they are needing it for with nothing out of their pockets.

Tell them in the letter that you will be calling them within the next five to ten days.

You must follow up with the phone call to make this strategy work. Even though you are practically going to be giving away free money, most people still won't call you back.

You have to make this as easy and painless as possible for the organization you're contacting.

When you call them go over the details with them. Most will see how easy it is for them to make some extra money for their organization, but you will still have a few that won't want to have to organize their group to hand out fliers or letters.

When you get them onboard, finalize what weekend or dates you will be allowing the letter to be turned in, and begin writing your letter so that it's appropriate for the organization you're working with.

If possible, try to have the organization pass out the letter no more than five to seven days before the event starts. Any more than seven days and the person who receives the letter could forget they have it when it comes time to redeem them.

You will find that most of the people that lead these organizations are not marketing people, so most of them will think that the more time they have to pass out the letters the better.

Their thoughts are that if they have a month to hand out letters, they can hand out twice as many letters and make twice as much money. Unfortunately this isn't the case, so try to convince them to keep it to one week, two weeks max.

You will have a few that will insist on a longer time period to hand the letters out. If they insist, let them have it their way. It's only costing you a few cents to print off several copies of the letter for them, so one sale is all you need to show a profit.

I always had the organization print off their own copies of the letters to pass out. Most of these organizations already had some type of commercial copier that they could use to print them as they needed them.

If you pay for the printing costs yourself of several hundred, or several thousand copies, then you run the risk of overprinting because you really won't know how many copies the organization will hand out, and you're also cutting into your profits by adding additional costs to this marketing campaign.

Better to let the organization handle their own printing. That way if the people handing out the letters get lazy, lose interest, or decide to trash a few hundred fliers, it won't come out of your pocket.

Never, if at all possible schedule two organizations letters on the same dates. Unless you have a really awesome crew, there will be confusion over which organizations letter is getting redeemed.

Let's look at the potential that this strategy has on your business.

If you could schedule two of these events every month at your store, and only had a small redemption rate on your letters, with each event bringing in only $800 in additional sales that would be an additional $19,200 every year in practically free money.

Your results would probably be a lot higher than $800 in sales if you team up with organizations with a large membership, but even if you only run less than $800 on this promotion, it's still <u>free money</u>.

Unless your donating more money than it costs you to make the pizza, or printing up the letters yourself, which I discourage, this is a can't lose strategy. You will make money using it.

On the next page is an example of a letter I wrote for one of my local church groups to pass out to raise money for church camp. Use it as a template to create your own letters for groups to use.

Dear neighbor,

Remember back when you were 13? Remember how great it felt to have the school year end and summer vacation start?

Do you remember getting to go to summer camp with your friends? Remember the excitement leading up to the first day of camp, the anticipation of hanging out with your friends for a whole week.

Well, that time is coming up for our kids at Pleasant View Baptist Church, unfortunately, several of these kids might be left out this year because of financial difficulties outside their control.

I can't imagine what these kids would feel like seeing their friends head off to camp while they have to stay at home. And one week at church camp can unlock more dreams than a whole year of classroom time can for these kids at this age.

They just need a little bit of money to help them get there.

Well – **Simple Simons Pizza** is stepping up to help raise the money for these kids.

And it's easy for you to help them out. They will donate $3.00 for every large pizza you order, or $2.00 for every medium pizza you order on June 8th, 9th, or 10th.

Just bring this letter in with you when you place your order. Or if you prefer to call in, just let them know that you have one. Their located at 125 Steve Berry Blvd., right across the street from Wal Mart. Their phone number is **825-5500**.

You'll get to enjoy oven fresh Simple Simons Pizza and at the same time – help make sure that none of these kids get left out this year.

So please, order your favorite pizza and help these kids out!

Thank you very much,

Gerald Pilant
Pleasant View Baptist Church

PS. Order any large or medium pizza from June 8th thru June 10th, present this letter when you place your order, and Simple Simons Pizza will donate part of every sale to help pay for these kids to go to church camp.

PPS. Use this letter as many times as you like between June 8th and June 10th!

For the fundraising letters, be sure to use the persons name that's leading or running the organization instead of your own name and signature.

<u>Everyone Wins Contest</u>

This is a sneaky low cost strategy that will give your store a quick shot in the arm of additional cash flow.

Everyone likes contests. Better yet, everyone likes winning contests.

Here's how this strategy plays out.

Have your printer make you up some business cards. About a thousand of these is all you will need. Color Printing Central can get you 1000 business cards printed up for around 65 bucks including shipping. You can get in touch with them at www.colorprintingcentral.com.

The front of the card will give details about the contest. Put on the top front of the card the words "GRAND PRIZE ELIGIBILITY CARD". Then have it say something like "Register to win 5 FREE pizzas!" Or whatever you want to give away for free.

On the back of the card, have a place for the customer to write in their name, address, and phone number, and be sure to put when the drawing will be held for the free pizzas.

Now have your staff and drivers pass these out to your customers that come into your store or order for delivery.

Black Ops Pizza Marketing

I have even had a few of my employees run across the street to the Wal-Mart parking lot with a hundred cards and put them on peoples windshields. Just makes sure you have their permission before you do this.

Some of the managers are really cool about it as long as you don't put them on the windshields of the employees cars, and others are literal parking lot Nazis, throwing their unlimited "Wal-Mart Manager Power" against whichever poor soul they deem unworthy.

Now when these cards are turned in, the first thing you need to do is enter their information into your data base if they're not already in there so you're growing your "herd". Don't get sloppy and think you can skip this part. Each new person that turns in a card could be worth several hundred dollars to you in future revenue.

So have your drawing, and get your winner.

Now we're going to go back and write a letter to all of the other people who entered the contest. This letter will reveal who won the contest, and also tell them that while they didn't win the grand prize…

…they did win the second place prize of any free appetizer of their choice on their next visit. They just need to bring in the letter to get their free appetizer.

Here is a template of what your letter should look like to mail to everyone who didn't win the grand prize.

Dear Friend,

My name is Paul Baker and I am the owner of the Simple Simons Pizza right here in Pryor.

The reason I'm writing is to thank you for entering my drawing for the five **FREE** pizzas. I'm sorry you didn't win the grand prize. That was won by Mr. and Mrs. Ronald Lefay and they really had a great time when they came in to collect.

However, I do have some good news because I am happy to inform you that you did win a valuable second prize! What you have won is any one of my mouth watering appetizers off our menu and, I will be happy to give it to you the next time you come in for dinner!

Thanks again for entering my little contest and I hope to see you soon.

Sincerely,

Paul Baker
Owner

P.S. Please bring this letter with you when you come in to collect your **FREE** appetizer and, it is necessary that you claim your prize sometime between now and the end of the month. Thanks again. I really appreciate having you as a customer.

Now let's look again at the numbers to see what potential this tactic has.

If you hand out 1000 entry cards, get half of those turned in, you've just potentially added 500 new names to your data base. That's a huge number of names. Now if out of those 500 that turned in their card, only half of those redeemed their second place letter…

At an average of $16.00 per order that's $4000 in sales. After subtracting $125 in postage and mailing costs (.50 each), $1,400 in food cost (35%), and $65 in printing costs for your cards, your left with a profit of **$2,410.00**.

That might not seem like a lot of money, but what if only 25 of those people that turned in their letters became regular customers, ordering only once every month? Now let's see what our yearly return is on this tactic.

25 new customers x $16.00 average order = $400
$400 x 12 months = $4800 sales per year

Subtract your 35% in food cost, and you're left with a profit of $3120 per year. Add that in with the profit that the actual contest generated and you're left with a yearly profit of **$5530**.

That might not initially sound like a lot of money for an entire year, but remember that your initial out of pocket investment to get that $5530 was only $190. $1590 if you wanted include food cost in there.

There's no reason why you couldn't run this promotion three or four times per year, which would then have the potential to triple that $5530.

<u>Referrals</u>

Most pizzeria owners completely overlook one of the most powerful sales building tools out there at their disposal. And that tool is referrals.

Most people don't think that you can "control" referrals. That it's just something that happens spontaneously from you doing a good job and someone telling their friends about you.

However, when you actually "engineer" a referral program in your restaurant, you can grow your business by leaps and bounds for year after year.

Let's look at why referrals are so powerful.

When you see all those high dollar ads in phone books, newspapers, direct mail or wherever, most of them all scream about how great they are or why they're the best.

When our senses get bombarded with that many advertisements day in and day out, we just don't believe the hype when someone tells us how great they are and we put our defenses up.

Now on the other hand, when a close friend or relative tells us how great something is, we pay attention. After all, it's someone close to us suggesting we try something because they like it, and they think we would like it as well.

When you actively start orchestrating and harnessing the powers of referrals in your pizzeria, you're going to quickly overtake your competitors.

So how do we actually take something that seems so random and uncontrollable as referrals and harness it into a revenue generating system?

It's not as hard as you might think. Here's how this tactic works.

When your customer calls in to place an order and gives their phone number, they're order history should show up on your point of sale system (you do have a point of sale system don't you?). The customers we're looking for are the ones who order frequently, or on a consistent basis.

After the order has been placed, you or your staff will say something similar to the following script.

"Thanks for your order tonight Janet. Could you do me a favor? I'm always looking to grow my business with new customers and was hoping that you might know a few people that you could refer that might like my pizza and become a great customer like you are. If you could bring in two names and addresses with you when you pick up your order, I'll give you a free order of garlic bread."

You could also have your delivery driver pick up the names and addresses when they delivered the pizza if they didn't pick up.

It's also important that you tell the customer that you are looking for people that might become great customers like them. This makes them feel important and special. It's also important that you give them some kind of free item to show your gratitude. I would even give them a free pizza every time they gave me potential customer names and addresses.

Now after you have your names and addresses, you're going to send these folks a personal letter, signed in blue ink by you, that says a mutual friend of yours (Janet in this instance) thought they might like your pizza so you want to give them one for free to try out.

I always put a dollar limit of $25 just so I wouldn't get someone trying to add 20 toppings to a pizza.

At this point, if you're like a lot of other pizzeria owners, you're thinking "I can't afford to give away free food, this is a crazy idea!"

But let's look at the potential numbers

If you or your crew only gets 5 people per day (this is a really low number) to give two names and addresses each, that's 10 names per day.

Your food cost on the free pizza you give to these 10 people is probably going to be around $2.50 each (yours will probably be lower than this), and the postage cost to mail the letters for the free pizzas will cost you roughly .50 each.

So at the end of the month if you're consistent with working your referrals, you're looking at around $900 in food cost and postage. (Remember this cost is going to be spread out over an entire month so you probably won't even notice this cost)

10 names per day x 30 days = 300 names
300 names x $3.00 (2.50 food cost and .50 postage) =
$900.00

I can imagine the sweat coming off your brow right now. You're getting nervous about this aren't you? Well… Here's why you can't afford not to do this.

Let's say that out of those 300 names that you give a free pizza to, only 10% of those become regular customers. That's only 30 out of 300. (This will probably be a lot higher since these people were recommended by a "mutual friend" but we'll keep the number low for now).

If those 30 customers become regular customers, ordering twice a month at an average ticket of $20.00 per order, **your $900 investment has just turned into $14,400 per year in sales!** That's not too shabby of an investment.

Now what if you can convert 20% of those 300? You would be looking at **$28,800 per year in additional sales**. See how incredibly profitable this can be?

And that's not taking into account the fact that after a few orders from these new "referrals" that you can then ask them for referrals. The system keeps building on itself.

Don't be afraid to use these two tactics to increase your cash flow overnight. Your competitors are going to be scared to raise their prices, and won't even think about orchestrating a referral system for their business.

Getting In Front Of The Decision Makers

Here's an "old school" marketing tactic that will get you in front of the decision makers when trying to drum up new business for your pizzeria.

From time to time you'll come across large businesses or organizations that would be profitable for you to cater, deliver, or partner with.

If you've ever tried to get past the "gatekeepers" and get to the decision maker, you know how difficult this can be.

You really can't blame these large companies though for having these gatekeepers, they are usually extremely busy, and are constantly bombarded by other businesses and salespeople trying to get their attention to use their services.

It can get really frustrating, especially when you know that if you get this catering account it could add thousands of dollars to your sales every year. Every time you call, the gatekeeper tells you that Mr. Bigwig is out of the office, or in a meeting.

What we're going to do with this tactic, is not only get you noticed by the decision maker, but actually have the decision maker want to call you.

Now while this tactic isn't foolproof, it does usually have a success rate of around 60%. So if you use this on 10 potential new accounts, you probably are going to end up with 5 or 6 of the accounts you're going after.

Here's how we're going to do this.

The first thing we need to do is to find an important date in the decision makers life. This can be their birthday, business anniversary, an award they just won, 30 years on the job, Christmas, whatever... we just need to tie this in to an important date if at all possible.

With today's technology and social sites like Facebook, this is a lot easier to do than it was 10 or 15 years ago, and by tying this tactic in with a specific date, it allows us a legitimate excuse to give someone that we don't personally know a gift.

So what we're going to do is call up the receptionist (this is usually the gatekeeper) and try to get her on our side. You'll tell the receptionist that you're wanting to buy Mr. Bigwig a birthday present (or whatever special date you use) and you are needing his shoe size, and was wondering if the receptionist could get it for you.

Now go out and purchase a $50-$100 dollar pair of shoes for Mr. Bigwig. Then you send Mr. Bigwig one of the shoes, not both of them, just one, with some kind of letter that says something like:

"Dear Mr. Bigwig, Hi, my name is Bob, I own a pizza restaurant that I think would be really beneficial and convenient for you and your company. Since I needed some way to get my "foot" in the door, I wanted to send you this shoe and have the opportunity to meet with you on Wednesday of next week. And when I show up, I'll bring you the other shoe."

Now what you do is you take the single shoe, and the letter you have written and have it delivered to Mr. Bigwig by Fedex with signature confirmation.

Using FedEx over the US Postal service gives your package a lot more impact, and increases the chances of it getting into the hands of the person you want it delivered to, so pay the extra to have it professionally delivered.

What will usually happen next, is Mr. Bigwig will call you because he wants the other shoe, which will allow you to get the meeting with him that you're wanting and give him your "sales pitch."

At the end of the day, people are all the same. It doesn't matter if you're a grocery clerk making eight dollars an hour, or a CEO of a company making three million a year. If you have one shoe, human nature makes us want the other one that goes with it.

This is also a great strategy for getting job interviews, and makes you stick out over all the other applicants.

How To Create Newspaper Ads For Maximum Profits

Ask almost any independent pizzeria owner, or any person wanting to start their own small business how they are going to advertise that business, and I would bet that almost 99% of them would respond with "I would advertise in the newspaper."

Sounds like a pretty good idea doesn't it? And actually, if you're already in business for yourself, you've probably already advertised in your local newspaper at least once, maybe even a few times.

Did you get a good response from your ad? Did the ad pay for itself? Did you even track the results from your ad to know if it was profitable?

I'm gonna bet that the answer is a resounding NO to all three of those questions. So let's go through how a newspaper ad is usually placed.

You know the drill… Your local newspaper ad rep comes in or calls to sell you an ad in their paper. What usually happens is that the ad always ends up looking like you just put a copy of your business card in the newspaper.

Or you just let the newspaper ad rep create an ad for you, which is absolutely crazy. Newspaper ad reps know how to sell ads – not create them so that they are profitable.

It's kinda like letting your local auto mechanic do your colonoscopy. Sure, he can probably get the job done, but it's going to be a lot more painful and you more than likely won't get the results you're looking for.

And as always, you're out the $200 or $300 bucks that it costs you to run the ad with very little if any increase in sales from it.

Then when you tell the ad rep that you didn't get any response from the ad, they give you repetition excuse, telling you that you need to keep running the ad so you get more exposure… well, people die from exposure, so don't buy into the repetition excuse that they give you.

Look, you'll find that most people in the pizza business are all running their newspaper ads the same way. And honestly… it was what I was doing when I first got started in the pizza business, and I'll bet it's what you've been doing when you advertise in the newspaper too.

Most pizzeria owners put out "professional looking" newspaper ads that all follow a similar formula. This "formula" is generally what I refer to as "name, rank and serial number" advertising.

These ads usually have a nice picture of your food or restaurant, it showcases your logo and has your phone number in big bold print. There might be a coupon on there as well for a couple bucks off, or a low priced offer. These ads are usually very neat, well arranged, and have lots of "white space". Sound familiar?

Check out this ad… it's typical "image advertising"… the kind of advertising 99.9% of pizza restaurants do that DOES NOT get good results:

ABC PIZZA

123 Anywhere Street
Anywhere City, State 54321

555-123-4567

$2.00 OFF Any Large Pizza!

Void with any other promotion or offer. Limit one coupon per visit per customer.

See, now that's a perfect example of "name, rank, serial number" image based newspaper ad, and that's how almost every business owner does their newspaper ads. You see, everyone simply follows the same formula all the other businesses and restaurants are following – the "formula" of image advertising… and their ads aren't doing squat.

In fact, just last year I was talking to a gentleman that owned his own small window tinting business. He had moved from the Los Angeles California area to Tulsa Oklahoma because he just couldn't afford the high cost of living in California.

After we got to talking, I found that he blamed the bad economy for his business not doing well, and the lack of customers. He told me that the last straw was when he placed an ad for his window tinting business in the Los Angeles Times newspaper and didn't get a single job from the ad.

Actually, he told me he didn't even get a single phone call from someone inquiring about window tinting from the ad. He said the ad cost him almost $1000 bucks and went out to **over 600,000 people**, and he got ZERO response!

He said that if his ad went out to that many people, and he didn't get a single job from the ad, then obviously the economy there was so bad that it was time to move on to somewhere else.

Now think about this. You have a newspaper ad that goes out to over 600,000 people, and no one even inquires about your service? **That's 600,000 people!** Don't you think that one or two people might want their windows tinted? Especially in sunny California?

Granted, I didn't see the ad, so I don't know what he put in it. And I don't know what the actual circulation for the Los Angeles Times is (I'm sure it's no small number). But I can almost guarantee his newspaper ad was similar to the example I showed you earlier.

Here's another example from my own personal experience.

The first February that I had my pizza store, my local newspaper ad rep called me and asked me if I wanted to place an ad for their "special" Valentine's day edition. She told me how this special edition had a really big readership and how my pizza business would be a perfect fit for this issue of the paper.

I was busy with what I thought was really important things at the time (like saucing pizzas) and told her I wasn't sure if I would have the time to create an ad before the deadline.

She told me no problem, just send me over a copy of my business card and she would take care of the rest. So that's what I did. When she was done, the ad looked really similar to the example I showed you earlier. It had my company logo, phone number, and some valentine hearts on it. It also had "show this ad for $2.00 off any large pizza" on it.

The ad ran, and guess what…

I didn't have a single person call in and use the $2.00 off coupon. The stupid ad cost me $150 and didn't make me a single penny in return. I would have gotten the exact same result if I had taken that $150 and flushed it down the toilet!

You know what the really funny thing is though… When I looked through that issue of the newspaper, almost every other business had the exact same ad as I did!
Name, phone number and some stupid red and pink hearts.

Listen closely! I'm going to repeat what I said earlier because it's so important. **Never let the newspaper ad rep create your ad!** They are there to sell you an ad, not bring you in customers.

There is a much better way to run your newspaper ads than the same way everyone else runs them. It's been shown through testing, that by making your ads <u>not</u> look like and actual ad, you'll get a better response.

You see when people are looking at ads, their defenses are up, they know you're trying to sell them something. Now if they read what they think is a news article on your restaurant, they don't have their defenses up, after all – it's just an article.

I'm going to say it again so it's perfectly clear.

<u>You want to create your newspaper advertisements so that they don't appear to be advertisements</u>.

What we're going to do is make our ad look as close to the editorial style of the newspaper we're advertising in as much as possible. Use the same font, same font size, same spacing, same layout, same everything!

Go get a current copy of the newspaper you're wanting to advertise in, and match up your ad to where it looks **exactly** like how they have their newspaper laid out.

Here is an example of what our ad should look like.

"Agave's Mexican Restaurant Serving Up Scale Quality Food At Family Friendly Prices"

Tulsa, OK – Located on 29th and Utica Street, Agave's Mexican Restaurant is serving up food that Is blatantly up scale, at prices that You can afford to feed your whole family on.

We stopped in to see what all the fuss was about and were amazed by the large spacious dining room, the enormous chandeliers, the inlaid table tops, and the decorative lighted columns. After looking over 54 different menu entrees we selected the filete de pescado and the pollo con camaron. The filete de pescado featured a grilled whitefish cooked perfectly so the fish was flaky and moist. It was served on a bed of crisp lettuce and surrounded by avocado, lime, and onion slices. It was also served with tender rice and the most authentic refried beans I've eaten in years.

The pollo con camaron included a deeply marinated chicken breast grilled to perfection, then topped with spinach, cheese, and seven plump grilled shrimp over a pool of cream sauce that will have your eyes rolling back into your head from pure delight. This dish was also served with the same surprisingly large portion of beans and rice that the filet de pescado came with and also included our choice of steamed vegetables. For dessert we opted for the moist brownie under a scoop of creamy vanilla ice cream. We were surprised to find that brownie was larger than expected and more than enough for both of us to share.

But the biggest surprise was when we went to pay for our meal. We honestly had thought a meal as upscale as this would set us back around forty dollars for the two of us, but it was less than twenty-five dollars! You owe it to yourself to try Agave's at least once, I promise you won't be disappointed.

If you want to contact them to make reservations (they do get really busy) you can call them at 918-000-0000.

And be sure to tell your waitress that you seen this article in this news paper and your appetizer is on the house.

Notice how the ad actually looks like an article in the paper? Now if you were trying to make a decision on where to go and eat out at on Friday night, and you saw this ad, and a competing ad sitting right next to it with another restaurants logo, telephone number, and goofy slogan like "you've tried the rest, now try the best" which would you be more inclined to visit?

Generally an ad like this will generate anywhere from 300%-700% more readership than other ads that are blatant "advertisements"

Notice at the top of the ad it says**PAID ADVERTISEMENT**? The newspaper will require you to put this above your ad so there's no "confusion" that it's an advertisement and not an actual editorial write up.

Putting the "paid advertisement" above your ad blatantly tells the reader that this is an ad, thus possibly hurting our response on the ad.

So what do we do?

Take a look at the ad now on the next page...

Black Ops Pizza Marketing

"Agave's Mexican Restaurant Serving Up Scale Quality Food At Family Friendly Prices"

Tulsa, OK – Located on 29th and Utica Street, Agave's Mexican Restaurant is serving up food that Is blatantly up scale, at prices that You can afford to feed your whole family on.

We stopped in to see what all the fuss was about and were amazed by the large spacious dining room, the enormous chandeliers, the inlaid table tops, and the decorative lighted columns. After looking over 54 different menu entrees we selected the filete de pescado and the pollo con camaron. The filete de pescado featured a grilled whitefish cooked perfectly so the fish was flaky and moist. It was served on a bed of crisp lettuce and surrounded by avocado, lime, and onion slices. It was also served with tender rice and the most authentic refried beans I've eaten in years.

The pollo con camaron included a deeply marinated chicken breast grilled to perfection, then topped with spinach, cheese, and seven plump grilled shrimp over a pool of cream sauce that will have your eyes rolling back into your head from pure delight. This dish was also served with the same surprisingly large portion of beans and rice that the filet de pescado came with and also included our choice of steamed vegetables. For dessert we opted for the moist brownie under a scoop of creamy vanilla ice cream. We were surprised to find that brownie was larger than expected and more than enough for both of us to share.

But the biggest surprise was when we went to pay for our meal. We honestly honestly thought a meal as upscale as this would set us back around forty dollars for the two of us, but it was less than twenty-five dollars! You owe it to yourself to try Agave's at least once, I promise you won't be disappointed.

If you want to contact them to make reservations (they do get really busy) you can call them at 918-000-0000.

And be sure to tell your waitress that you seen this article in this news paper and your appetizer is on the house.

Did you pick up on this slick trick?

As you can see the **PAID ADVERTISEMENT** still appears in our ad, however you'll notice upon closer inspection that we have camouflaged the required **PAID ADVERTISEMENT** words with two bogus ads that are placed right below the required disclaimer.

So now our "real" ad is separated from those two potentially sales killing words and looks like real editorial content in the newspaper.

Pretty sneaky… huh.

Now running this kind of ad will probably cost you a little bit more than just paying to put your business card in the paper, but the results are well worth it.

When creating your ad, be sure to use descriptive words. Don't just put something like "Agave's has good food." That's not very stimulating. Make your reader imagine themselves already in your restaurant with their plate in front of them.

Be descriptive of all the smells, and taste. Make your readers really <u>desire</u> to visit your business.

And be sure to add in some kind of offer so you can track how well your ad is doing. This can be almost anything. Free appetizers, free drinks, free whatever. Just make sure you have the ability to track how much business the ad is pulling in.

Newspapers come in all kinds of shapes and sizes when it comes to advertising space. But there are a few "SAU's" which stands for "Standard Advertising Units" that you can get the most bang for your buck on.

These are full page ads. Horizontal half page ads. Vertical half page ads. Or a more or less square shaped ¼ page ad.

Full Page Ad

Two Horizontal ½ Page A

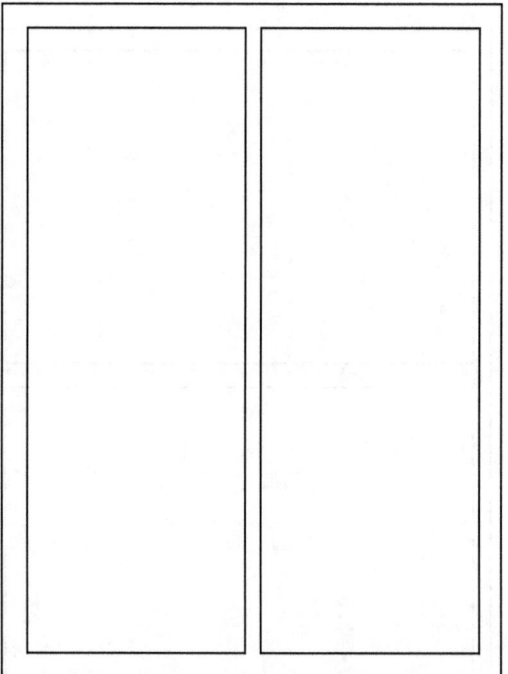

Two Vertical ½ Page Ads

4 ¼ Page Ads

Of these four Standard Advertising Units, everything else being equal, dollar-for-dollar, the most cost effective block of space where you'll get the most "bang for your buck" is the half page vertical.

This position insures that your headline will be above the fold of the newspaper and depending on your ad, will usually pull around 70% of what a full page ad will pull. So you're paying for half the space, and only losing only around 30% of what you would have had if you had ran a full page ad.

Now if you have enough <u>good copy</u> for a full page ad… then use a full page ad! The quarter page ads work too, but you can expect to only pull in about 25% of what a good full page ad will pull, or 50% of what a good half page ad will pull.

Try to stay away from the bottom half of the horizontal ½ page ad, and the two bottom halves of the ¼ page ads. Your ad will be below the fold and won't pull as much as the other spots.

Ok, so now you know the correct way to place your ad so that you're pulling maximum profits from them. No longer will you be wasting your hard earned money on lame business card ads with your logo and phone number plastered on them.

Now, as an added bonus, I'm gonna show you a sneaky way to get your newspaper ads printed for a fraction of what it would normally cost you to place the ad.

Here's what we're gonna do. Get your ad ready for printing and contact your ad rep for the newspaper your advertising in. Show them the ad, and inquire about how much it's going to cost you to place the ad.

Obviously depending on where in the country you're located, and the size of distribution of the newspaper, the cost could vary greatly. So we're going to say that our ad is going to cost $1000 to place.

She quotes you the $1000 price. At this point you need to explain to here that you only have a $600 budget to place your ad. She will most likely tell you that you won't be able to place the ad at that price.

This is fine.

While on the phone, make sure that you get the name of the person you're dealing with and if you don't have it, get the newspapers mailing address.

Then mail the ad, along with a check for the $600 to the person you spoke to. Better yet, if it's a small local newspaper, send it to the owner of the newspaper.

Send a letter along with the check and the ad explaining that while you understood what the actual cost of the ad is, you only have the $600 (or $500, $400, whatever), to spend on advertising. And that should they happen to find some "extra room" for the ad before going to print, then to please run the ad and cash the check.

This is where the emotional magic kicks in.

By actually sending a real check to the decision maker, you've put them in the position of emotionally feeling like their "losing" money by sending the check back to you.

The newspaper owner now has to give you back $600 if they decide not to run your ad. Emotionally that is going to feel like they just missed out on $600 bucks. That's $600 bucks that was in their grubby little paws... then gone if they don't agree to run the ad.

I remember having a church come in to my pizza store on Friday evening and pre pay for 20 large pizzas for a church yard sale their youth group were going to have on Saturday.

It poured down sheets of rain that next day and they had to cancel the yard sale. When I had to give them a refund for the 20 pizzas (it was just a little over a hundred bucks) it felt like I had just lost that money.

Once that money is in your hands, it's really difficult to emotionally let it go.

Now admittedly this strategy won't work for every newspaper and won't work every time you attempt to use it.

If you're trying to place an ad in a gigantic newspaper and the decision maker is a minimum wage idiot in a cubicle scratching their head with an ink pen, then it probably won't work.

Some of these "cubicle idiots" are not allowed to think at all. If you were to send them a check for $49,998 for a full page ad, and their little computer screen told them the ad price was $50,000. They would more likely than not send back your $49,998 check and tell you to send a check for the full amount before the ad is placed.

How To Get Free Publicity

Most pizza store owners don't realize that they're missing out on the one form of advertising that can absolutely launch their business into new levels of income that they never imagined they could attain.

This type of advertising that they overlook is publicity!

Publicity is an extremely powerful form of advertising that is fun, easy, and very profitable. It can very quickly raise your sales regardless of whether your store is already cranking out great sales numbers, or whether you're trying to turn around a store that's not performing like it should.

And best of all, getting publicity is free! You will no longer have to pay extremely high advertising prices to newspapers and radio stations to get your business promoted by them.

By the time you get done going through this course, you'll know how to have the newspapers and radio stations calling you!

It's extremely simple to get free publicity, the problem is, most businesses don't know how to play the publicity game. Yes, I said game. Getting publicity is a game, **and if you don't know how to play the game, you will never get any type of publicity whatsoever!**

You're about to learn how to play the publicity game by going through this course. Once you see how it's done, and are made aware of the mistakes that 99% of pizza stores make when trying to get publicity, you will be able to use publicity to your advantage against your competitors.

Just imagine going through your local newspaper and seeing one of your competitors coupons or ads, then turning the page and seeing a half page article written about you and your store.

You're competitor probably paid three or four hundred dollars to get their ad placed there, you got a half page write up... for free!

You then turn on your radio and hear your competitors radio commercial playing. They probably paid over a thousand dollars for that spot a few times a day. You then hear yourself being interviewed by a local talk show host about your business and this cost you... absolutely nothing!

You then turn on your nightly local news station on your television and see your competitors television ad running. God knows how much they paid for that 30 second spot. But then you see your local news reporter interviewing you about your pizza store on the 6:00 news... and this once again cost you nothing!

Think you can't get this kind of publicity for your pizza store? Think again. And getting this free publicity for your pizza store is easy! You just have to know how to play the game!

Not only is publicity free, but it also gives your pizza store instant credibility. When someone sees a write up about you in the paper, or hears you on the radio, you're instantly taken more seriously than you were before.

For instance, which sounds more credible? A big chain running a fifteen second radio commercial talking about how great their pizza is, or a local talk show host interviewing someone for five minutes about how to make a great pizza?

The guy being interviewed by a talk show host is a lot more credible than someone blowing their own horn about how great they are.

You also become a type of celebrity in your local community when you start getting publicity, and people love doing business with local celebrities.

You might be thinking that this sounds too good to be true, but I assure you that if you follow the rules in this book, your chances of getting publicity for your pizza store will be much higher than everyone else trying to get publicity for theirs.

But I need to be up front with you. This is not a get rich quick scheme. There is work and effort involved in getting publicity, and unfortunately, if you don't put in the time and effort, it probably won't work for you.

It's like everything else in life, the more you use it, the better at it you'll get.

So if you're ready to get free publicity for your pizza store, then let's get started.

Your Story Ideas

I'm going to immediately start with one of the biggest misconceptions that pizza store owners have about publicity. And that is that they don't have a story to tell.

Most owners think that a reporter won't touch their story unless it involves some super star, or unless you have something super exciting to tell.

This is simply not true. Go through your local newspapers and watch your local news channels. What are most of them about? Probably local community events and local elections.

There's probably some articles about how to do something like make great colored easter eggs around easter time, or how to trim your trees in the spring, or how the city mayor is planning to handle the new sidewalk construction, etc…

These are not super star stories, however they are the kind of stories that get ran every day.

This is something you have to keep in mind.

Reporters have a job. Their job is to find interesting stories to run in their newspapers, on their radio stations, and in their television stations every single day.

The newspapers for instance have to find enough interesting stories to fill their newspapers every day of the week that they print one, and this is tough to do.

Reporters are hungry for any story that may be interesting to their readers.

Your story doesn't have to be anything with star power or filled with nonstop excitement. You could just do a simple story on how to make your own pizza at home, or the correct way to put the toppings on a pizza before cooking it.

You could explain why delivery drivers have the fifth most dangerous job in the world according to the U.S. Bureau of Labor Statistics, or a story on how to toss dough like a professional.

See how simple this information is? There's nothing exciting or crazy about these stories, but they are almost sure to get publicity. These are interesting stories that the reporter can pass on to their audience.

And now here comes the first big secret to getting free publicity for your pizza store...

When you're coming up with your story, you always want to tell, not sell! Never, under any circumstances try to sell your product when creating your story. The reporter is not interested in you trying to sell a pizza.

If your story involves you selling yourself or product in any way shape or form, your story will go into the trash. This is where the game begins.

The reporter wants and needs good interesting stories. They want to look good in the eyes of their audience. By writing about how the local pizza shop is having a half price sale, they're not creating anything interesting for their readers.

If your story has even the slightest hint of a sales pitch, the reporter will be thinking "Go buy an ad pal" and will toss your story into the round filing cabinet.

Do not under any circumstances try to sell. This is what most pizza stores do when trying to get a story run in a newspaper, radio, or television. They try to pitch their product, then wonder why the reporter doesn't have any interest in them.

So now you're probably wondering "So how do I sell my product if I don't ever mention that I'm selling it," well, here's the best way to describe what happens.

You probably have seen some of those big television shows that are like Oprah or some other television show. The host will usually have some kind of guest on their program. On this particular episode, the host has a fitness expert on named Gary.

This guest shows the hosts audience for the next hour how to cook healthy nutritious meals that will help you lose weight, and shows you different exercises that will shred the fat off of you and give you rock hard abs in only a few months.

Almost at the end of the show, the host and the Gary will be talking some more about different health foods that burn fat fast, when the host will interrupt the guest and say something like…

"Could I interrupt you for a second please Gary"… The host will then look at the camera and say… "Folks, you've been watching my show for a really long time now, and you all know how much I've been struggling with my weight. Well, a few weeks ago Gary sent me a copy of his new book How to have awesome abs in only 90 days, and since I've read and implemented his cooking and exercise program, I've lost over 18 pounds in just two weeks! Folks if you don't get a copy of Gary's new book, then don't you complain to me when you don't look good in that new bathing suit this summer... Gary, I'm sorry for interrupting you, please go ahead with what you were saying..."

Cha Ching!

That's the game. You give the reporter interesting information that will make them look good for their audience, they in turn will sell your product for you.

What if our fitness expert Gary, during his interview kept saying something like... "You can see the proper way to do crunches in my new book on page 38" or "All the recipes I'm showing you can be found in my new book, available at Amazon.com."

The instant he tries to pitch his book, he loses all credibility. He's just become a salesman, not an expert on the subject giving away free information to help people out.

Let the reporter sell for you! They will always do a much better job of selling your product to their audience than you will.

So to get started, make a list of all the potential stories you can think of for your pizza store. Don't worry if it seems like your story might be boring or you think everyone already knows what you're thinking about telling.

How long should you let your dough rise before its ready to make a pizza? You may know exactly how long, but most other people wouldn't have a clue. How thick should you pepperonis be sliced to avoid having them "cup" up in the oven? You might know, but no one else does.

Once you have a story, you will need to send out your press release on it, so let's get started on writing a press release that won't get trashed by the reporter.

Writing Your Press Release

Writing your press release is the first step in showing the reporter that you know how to play the game. There are certain rules that must be followed. If you break any of these rules, your press release will go into the trash.

Most people believe that the press release is the whole process of getting publicity, they just send out the press release and their done. This is completely untrue.

The press release is vitally important, but it's not the whole process to getting the publicity you want. In fact, the press release has only a small, but very important job.

The only job of the press release is to get the reporters attention.

That's its only job, and you must follow a certain format when writing your press release or you will immediately let the reporter know that you don't know how to play the publicity game.

Let's get started.

You will always put your press release on a standard 8.5 x 11 sheet of white paper.

Always use white, always 8.5 x 11. Never change this. The reporter doesn't want to see a press release on a green sheet of paper.

Your press release will <u>always</u> be on one sheet of paper, and one sheet only. If you send the reporter a press release with two or more pages, you're letting the reporter know that you don't know how to play the game.

In the top left corner of your press release, you will put one of two things there. You will put the phrase FOR IMMEDIATE RELEASE or you will use a similar phrase with a time limit on it like FOR RELEASE ON OR BEFORE CHRISTMAS 2012.

This lets the reporter know that when they get your press release, they can either use it immediately and anytime they want, or if there's a date that the story needs to be ran before, it lets them know that as well.

So let's touch on the FOR IMMEDIATE RELEASE first.

By putting this in the upper left hand corner of your press release, the reporter knows that there's no time qualifications on this press release. They know that they would be able to use it immediately, or later.

If you had a story about how to throw and toss pizza dough like a professional, this story would be viable today, or a few months later, there's no time limit on the story that would make it ineffective.

Now if you were putting out a press release telling about how the president of the United States was going to be coming to eat at your pizza restaurant on October 7th of 2012, then you would put in the upper left corner

FOR RELEASE ON OR BEFORE
OCTOBER 7TH 2012

See how the time qualifier is relevant to the story. If the reporter were to wait till after October 7th to run the story, it would be old news.

Now most of the stores you probably do will not be having a time qualifier, they will probably mostly be general interesting information stories, however if you're doing a release about a fundraiser on certain days, or an event that's taking place on Christmas, you will need to use a time qualifier.

Now on the upper right side of the page, you need to have the following phrase…

FOR FURTHER INFORMATION CONTACT:
PAUL BAKER – (000) 555-1234

That's the only thing that will go in the upper right hand corner of your press release. You must give the reporter the name, and direct number to the person that will be answering the questions about the press release.

Never put down "for further information contact Bobs Pizza at 000-123-1234. The reporter needs the exact name of the person they need to contact.

The phone number needs to go directly to the contact person. Don't list your store number and have your employees answer it. The reporter must have the name and phone number of the contact person.

You can have your voice mail or answering machine get the call if the reporter tries calling you, however, you need to have a message that lets the reporter know that they got the right person.

A simple message like "Hi, you've reached Paul Baker, leave a message and I'll return your call within the hour"

If you're having the reporter call your home phone, make sure you don't have your five year old leaving a cute message on the machine. The reporter must know they have reached the right person, or they will not follow up on your press release.

Make sure you call the reporter back <u>that day</u>. Often time, the reporter is on a deadline to get their papers filled and might be needing your story to fill that slot for the next days paper. If you wait until the last minute, the reporter might have ran out of time to get the story written.

So what we have now is in the upper left corner your time qualifier, and in the upper right your contact information. Let's move on to the headline.

Your Press Release Headline

Your headline, like most headlines used in sales letters have one purpose and one purpose only, and that's to get the reporters attention.

Never write a press release with a headline that talks about your business. Doing this clues in the reporter that you don't know how to play the game, and your release will end up in the trash again.

Here's some really terrible headlines as an example that would go right into the trash.

Big Bobs Pizza Announces a 65% Increase In Sales

Big Bobs Pizza Offers 20% Off Discount

Big Bobs Pizza Adds New Lunch Buffet And Increases Menu Size

These are really bad headlines and are leading candidates for the reporter to make paper airplanes out of and crash into the trash can. They are all blatant sales pitches.

Take your time and write a good headline. Don't just think locally, think what headline would grab a reporters attention even if that reporters office was three states away.

Use the who cares tactic for writing headlines. If you can ask the question "who cares" and the answer is a lot of people, then you're onto a good headline. In the examples above, the only person that really cares is probably just Bob.

Now by far the easiest way to create a headline for a press release is to use a template.

I've included several template headlines that you can use to create your own headlines. Just take out the underlined words, and add your own. It's that easy. These are also great examples if you are looking for inspiration to create your own headlines from scratch.

Five Ways To Make Your Own Pizza Almost Instantly

Seven Secrets For Tossing Dough Like a Pro

Three No Fail Strategies For Quick and Easy Pizza Dough

A Little Mistake When Ordering A Pizza That Can Cost You A Fortune

A Little Mistake That Could Ruin Your Pizza Dough Almost Instantly And What You Can Do About It

A Startling Fact About Pizza Delivery Drivers

A New Way To Cook Pizza That Has Never Failed

How To Avoid The 7 Biggest Mistakes People Make When Making Pizza At Home

How To Get Other People To Pay For Your Pizza

How To Get Your Order Place At The Front Of The Line When Ordering Pizza

How To Toss Dough Almost Overnight

How To Think Like A Restauant Owner – The Two Things You Must Do

How To Transform Your Homemade Pizza into a Masterpiece

Latest Updated Information On The Dangers Pizza Delivery Drivers Face

What Everyone Should Know About Having A Pizza Delivered

Black Ops Pizza Marketing

See how easy it is to create your own headlines for your press release. Let's start creating our own press release using one of these headlines. We'll borrow from the "A startling fact about pizza delivery drivers.

Then lets drop the "pizza delivery drivers, and add in "The Dangers Pizza Delivery Drivers Face Every Day"

So our headline should read…

The Startling Facts About The Dangers Pizza Delivery Drivers Face Every Day

With this headline, you're letting the reporter know that you have something interesting that they could pass onto their audience, and it's not a sales pitch.

Now you don't want to let the reporter know what these dangers are just yet. You just want to arouse the curiosity of the reporter so they will be inclined to call you for more information.

So this is what our press release should look like so far…

FOR IMMEDIATE RELEASE   FOR FURTHER INFORMATION CONTACT
                                         PAUL BAKER – (123) 123-1234

The Startling Facts About The Dangers Pizza Delivery Drivers Face Every Day

So now the reporter knows that the press release can be used anytime, has your contact information, and will see a headline that catches their attention and forces them to keep reading.

Now we need to start working on the body copy. The body copy itself is broken down into three parts. The first part being basically your entire story compacted down into no more than three sentences.

This is another part of the game. <u>Under no circumstances do you want to go over three sentences</u>. If the reporter reads over these two or three sentences, they should have a good idea of what your press release is about.

If you don't think you can do this, think again. Look at the World War II for instance, you can sum up entire war by saying "we fought Hitler, we won. You need to do the same thing for this section of your press release.

So for our press release, we could compact our whole story into these two sentences.

"Every day thousands of pizza delivery drivers hit the road delivering pizza to their customers as quickly as possible. Criminals know that delivery drivers have food and cash with them, making them a prime target to be robbed, beaten, or even killed."

That's the whole story condensed down into two sentences. This is what you will have to do with your story. By writing more than three sentences, your letting the reporter know that you don't know how to play the game.

Let's jump to the second part of your press release.

The second part of your press releases body copy should quote yourself, and include your credentials. You should always quote yourself, never quote someone else, this could be confusing to the reporter.

By quoting someone else, the reporter may begin to wonder who this story is actually about, and it draws attention away from you. If you want to quote a relevant study or report, that's fine, but never quote someone else.

You might be thinking that you don't have any credentials that you can put in your press release. Fortunately for you, you have lots of credentials. You don't need to have a PhD, or a masters in business to have credentials.

Just look at what you're an expert at now. If you have pizza delivery drivers at your store, you've probably at one time or another had to do a few deliveries yourself, this gives you first hand knowledge.

You've had your pizza restaurant for nine years, you've seen which delivery drivers are safest and which are an accident waiting to happen.

You probably know which part of town your drivers are most likely to get robbed.

The point is, is that you can use almost anything as a credential. If you witnessed an accident, that can be a credential. If you were a victim of a robbery, that's a credential. If you own a business, that too is a credential.

You can use almost anything as a credential as long as it's relevant to the subject that you're discussing with the reporter. What you're trying to do here in the second part of your body copy is tell the report why you're qualified to talk about the subject in your press release.

So the second part of the body copy of our press release would look something like this...

"Most people don't realize that pizza delivery drivers put their lives on the line everyday just like police and firefighters do" explains Paul Baker who has owned several pizza restaurants and has done over 1000 pizza deliveries himself over the past nine years. "Pizza delivery is ranked as the fifth most dangerous job in the nation according to the U.S. Bureau of Labor Statistics, and most of these drivers make less than $15,000 per year."

So here, we've quoted ourselves, and listed our credentials. Now the reporter knows that we're qualified to talk about the subject in the press release.

So now we need to start on the third part of our body copy.

The third part of our body copy is the call to action for the reporter. Here we are going to use some bullets to tell the reporter why they should call you for an interview, and then give the reporter your contact information once again.

Your bullets need to catch the reporters attention again and compel them to call you to get more information about your story, then you need to let the reporter know what they will find out when they call you. Here's how the last section of your press release should look.

Paul can tell you audience:

- Why pizza delivery drivers are considered easy targets for criminals

- Why you want to keep your grass mowed, and lights on at night when having pizza delivered

- Why delivery drivers are not allowed to go inside your home when delivering

- Why some drivers won't deliver to certain neighborhoods

- How delivery drivers can protect themselves and prevent most crimes before they occur.

See how the bullets don't answer a question or reveal to much about the story, they create more interest, causing the reporter to want to call you to get more information.

Now we need to call the reporter to action. This can be as simple as the following:

"To get more information about the dangers pizza delivery drivers face, contact Paul Baker at (123) 123-1234"

The exact wording on this section isn't too important, you just want the reporter know that you have more good information on the subject and that you're available for interviews.

Very Important. When typing your press release, you always want to double space the entire body copy. Once again, another hint to the reporter that you know what's going on. This might look like it's too spaced out, but sometimes the reporter may want to jot down some notes in between the lines. This allows them to do so.

If your press release is all single spaced, it will make you look like a novice, and drastically reduce your chances of getting an interview. This is probably the most violated rule that people break when writing their press release.

And remember, at no point in your press release do we want to try to sell anything. Any attempt at selling will cause your press release to go into the trash.

So we have the correct information in the upper left corner and the upper right corner. We have our headline, and we have the three parts to our body copy. There's only one thing left to finishing up our press release, and it's another one of those secrets that lets the reporter know that you know how to play the publicity game.

At the very bottom of the press release you're going to put the pound symbol "#" three times. This is what journalists use, and lets the reporter know that they have reached the end of the press release and there's no more pages.

If you leave this off, the reporter may think that there's additional pages that are missing from the release, and not being able to find them, toss the page that they have into the trash.

Reporters don't have time to hunt for missing pages, if they think the entire press release isn't there, they will toss it and move on to the next story. Here's what the bottom of your page should look like.

# # #

On the next page is a copy of what our entire press release should look like when finished.

Black Ops Pizza Marketing

FOR IMMEDIATE RELEASE

FOR FURTHER INFORMATION CONTACT:
PAUL BAKER – (123) 123-1234

The Startling Facts About The Dangers Pizza Delivery Drivers Face Every Day

Every day thousands of pizza delivery drivers hit the road delivering pizzas to their cutomers as quickly as possible. Criminals know that delivery drivers have food and cash on them, making them a prime target to be robbed, beaten, or even killed.

"Most people don't realize that pizza delivery drivers put their lives on the line every day just like police and firefighters do" explains Paul Baker who has owned several pizza restaurants and has done over 1000 pizza deliveries himself over the past nine years. "Pizza delivery is ranked the fifth most dangerous job in the nation according to the U.S. Bureau of Labor Statistics, and most of these drivers make less than $15,000 per year."

Paul can tell your audience:

- Why pizza delivery drivers are considered easy targets for criminals
- Why you want to keep your grass mowed, and lights on when having pizza delivered
- Why delivery drivers are not allowed to go into your home when delivering
- Why some drivers wont deliver to certain neighborhoods
- How delivery drivers can protect themselves and prevent most crimes before they occur

To get more information about the dangers pizza delivery drivers face everyday, contact Paul Baker at (123) 123-1234

# # #

234

Use this press release as a template for your own press releases. Just be sure that you're never blatantly trying to sell something in them.

Your Biography Sheet

As you probably noticed, your press release, while very important, only has a small job, and that is to get the attention of the reporter.

Most people when trying to get publicity send out a press release and think that's all they need to do. Unfortunately, these people rarely ever get the reporter to call them, much less get the interview they're wanting.

The second sheet you will need to have is a biography sheet. In a later section of this course I'll show you exactly why you need this, but for now, let's practice writing one.

The biography sheet is similar to your press release in that you will again be using a plain white sheet of paper that's 8 ½ x 11" with no letter head, logos, or fancy graphics.

Like the press release, your biography sheet has only one job, and that is to tell the reporter why you're qualified for them to do the interview with you.

One difference in the biography sheet and the press release format, is that the biography sheet can be single spaced if you like. In fact, most of them are. The reporter will rarely take notes on your biography sheet, so whichever spacing you prefer will be fine.

The most important things to list on your biography sheet is your experience. If you've been in business for nine years, put that down. If you've ran multiple stores, put that down too.

If you went to college to learn business or a culinary art, that's good information to put down as well. Any college education, certification, or specific training in your field is ok to put into your biography sheet.

What you don't want to put down is your life history. The reporter doesn't care where you went to school, what your grade point average was, or any other of your life history, unless its directly related to your story.

It's also a good idea to put any story related results into your biography sheet that you may have. An example of this would be if you implemented a new delivery driver safety program in your stores that have reduced the risk of drivers being robbed or injured by 67%.

All the biography sheet is doing, is convincing the reporter that you know what you're talking about.

Testimonials are another good item to put into your biography sheet, but make sure that once again they are relevant to the story.

You couldn't have a testimonial from a happy customer saying "Paul makes the greatest pizzas, and his prices are awesome!"

While it's a nice testimonial, it's irrelevant to the story.

A good testimonial would be one from a delivery drivers wife who said something like...

"Because of the new safety procedures Paul implemented into his stores, my husband, who works part time for him, was kept from delivering to an empty house where a gang member was waiting to rob him as part of his gang initiation." Linda Berkshire

See how that testimony ties in with your story, these are great to include if you have them.

Another type of testimony to include is testimonies from other reporters who have interviewed you. These testimonies make the reporter looking over your story feel at ease knowing you have been interviewed before and know whats going on.

If they see another reporter praising you for an excellent interview, they are more likely to want to interview you themselves.

Starting out, you most likely won't have any testimonies to put in your biography sheet, and that's ok. Just start adding two or three to your biography sheet as you collect them.

The easiest way to get these testimonies is simply to ask the reporter for the testimony. Often times radio stations will praise you on the air about how great you are. Just ask the host if it's ok to use what he said as a testimony. He'll usually tell you that's why he said it.

Even if your testimonies are from tiny newspapers or radio stations, still put them on your biography sheet. As your testimonies start coming from bigger and bigger media outlets, simply replace the smaller testimonies with the ones from the bigger named papers and talk shows.

Black Ops Pizza Marketing

So here is our practice biography sheet that we will use.

PAUL BAKER
(123) 123-1234

Biography Sheet:
Paul Baker

Paul has been a multi store pizza restaurant operator for over nine years. In that time he has sold and delivered thousands of pizzas to local customers. His unconventional marketing strategies have launched his restaurant sales to over 314% in just under three years.

In addition to owning several pizza restaurants, Paul has also authored several books on sales and marketing, and has written numerous manuals on pizza delivery driver safety and procedures.

Paul's knowledge of his subject is through and his expression is opinionated and passionate. His interview style is captivating to both the interviewer and the audience, and he always shares insider tips and helpful ideas that his audience can get an immediate benefit from.

Paul's work has been praise by many in the pizza delivery industry:

"Thanks for the great information. One tip I learned from you enabled me to make a minor change in my pizza delivery policy, and saved me a lot of time and hassle"
Bob Jacobs- Bobs Pizza and Subs

"Because of the new safety procedures Paul implemented into his stores, my husband, who works part time for him was kept from delivering to an empty house where a gang member was waiting to rob him as part of his gang initiation"
Linda Berkshire-Vinita Ok

To book an interview, call (123) 123-1234

# # #

Notice that you still want to put your name and contact phone number in the top left corner of the page, and just like the press release, we will also include the pound sign three times at the end of the page.

Your Question and Answer Sheet

The last thing you will need is a question and answer sheet. This sheet could possibly be the most important part of getting a reporter to take your story, and very few people ever use one.

Here is why it is so important.

A reporter really doesn't know about the subject you're talking about. That may strange to you because you deal with what's involved with your story probably almost every day, however the reporter doesn't.

It would be like someone asking you to do a report on how to shave a poodle. The groomer that shaves poodles probably thinks "everyone knows that you have to bath a poodle before cutting their hair, then you always start from the feet and work your way up when shaving the dog." Because the groomer shaves poodles every day, its common knowledge to them, but you don't have a clue how it's done.

Same thing with reporters. They see that you sell pizzas every day, but honestly have no clue how the dough is made, how the dough needs to rise, how long to cook the pizza, how much cheese to put on one, etc…

So when they are reporting on a story, they need to have this information to be able to ask you the questions. So they have to do research, and find questions to ask you.

When you supply the reporter with a question and answer sheet, you have just done the reporters job for them, and they will love you for it!

When you get down to it, the reporter doesn't want to have to do all this research and paperwork to find out about your story. What they want is to be able to look good in the eyes of their audience.

It's like us going to work every day. Do we get excited about making pizzas? Nope, we get more excited about the end result, handing the customer their pizza and collecting the money.

By having a question and answer sheet ready, you have allowed the reporter to bypass a lot of the work, and get right to the end result.

Here's another way to look at it. Pretend its three minutes until your store closes. You only have enough time to make one more pizza, and two people walk in the door. (ya, I know any real pizza owner would sell to both people, but play along so I can make a point)

The first person walks in with a pizza already completely made. They tell you that they made this at home, and their power went off right when they were about to throw it into the oven. They tell you that they will pay you full price just for running it through your oven for them.

The second person wants to order a pizza from you, but wants you to make it like you normally do. You'll have to get the dough, sauce it, cheese it, and all the other things you have to do to get the pizza in the oven.

Now if you could only pick one customer to service, which would you pick? The first one has obviously done all the work for you and would be the easier of the two to service.

This is what the reporter sees as well, but they don't have to worry about pissing someone off if they don't want to run their story.

If a reporter is looking at two press releases from two pizza stores, and both stores are trying to get publicity for the same story, and one has a question and answer sheet, and the other doesn't, it's easy to see who is going to get the story ran.

Why would the reporter want to have to do all the research and think up some questions for one store owner, when the other one provided them with the questions they needed?

And there's more good news about your question and answer sheet.

It makes your interview a piece of cake! 99% of the time, the reporter will go straight down the list of questions you provided them.

This allows you to control the interview, you don't have to worry about the reporter asking you a question you might not have an answer to. If you wrote the questions… you should know the answers!

If you don't have a question and answer sheet, the reporter will have to create their own questions, and you'll never know what question is coming next. If the reporter starts asking questions about a topic you don't want to go talk about, it could end up being a rough interview.

Now if a reporter does ask a question that you don't know the answer to there's no problem with telling them you don't know the answer. For instance, if the reporter asks you "What would happen if you mixed lemon juice with your pizza sauce?"

You would simply need to tell the reporter "That's a good question, I've never tried making a pizza with lemon juice in my sauce. When I get back to the store today, I'll make a pizza with lemon juice in the sauce and get back with you and let you know how it turned out."

The reporter doesn't expect you to know absolutely everything about your topic, they just need to know that you're qualified to talk about it.

When creating your questions, there are certain rules you need to follow.

They absolutely <u>cannot</u> have simple yes and no answers. If you only give the reporter yes or no answers to your questions you're going to have a really short interview, and probably have blown any chances in the future of getting any more interviews from this reporter.

Your questions need to arouse the curiosity of the reporter and their audience. If you're questions are dry and uninteresting, you're probably not going to be getting too many more interviews.

Don't worry about how long your answers should be to your questions. Just give as much information as is needed to answer the question without rambling on about it. If you talk too long about a certain question, the reporter will interrupt you and lead you into the next question.

So let's get to writing our practice question and answer page.

Same format as our other press release and biography sheet. 8 ½ x 11 sheet of white paper, one page only.

In the upper right corner, we will put **Contact Number: (123) 123-1234**. We want our contact number right there in front of the reporters face in case they need to call us with a question so they don't have to hunt for your phone number on one of the other sheets.

Then we will create our headline. Since we are dealing with the dangers pizza delivery drivers face, our headline will look something like this...

Suggested interview Questions For Paul Baker Oklahomas Leading Authority On Delivery Driver Safety

We could have just stopped at the first sentence, and not added the "oklahomas leading authority on delivery driver safety," but when we add in our credentials, it gives the reporter some idea on what we will be talking about.

<u>Don't be afraid to call yourself an expert or an authority</u> on your subject. Most people are afraid to call themselves any type of expert on what they do. But the fact of the matter is... They are an expert! At the very least, an authority on the subject.

You probably know more than most people do about your subject, and if you're not an authority on your subject, why would the reporter be talking to you?

Even your grandmother could be considered an expert on baking cookies! You don't need to have someone else call you an expert or authority on something before you can start using that title. You know your stuff, you already are an expert, use the title!

So we have our headline, now we're going to start on our questions. The number of questions you put on your question and answer sheet isn't too important. Just make sure that the question and answer sheet doesn't begin to look too crowded.

So if you have 20 questions for the reporter to ask, and the page looks crowded, cut it down to 15 or 17 questions. If it still looks crowded, cut a few more.

If possible, your first question needs to be one that challenges you. Not meaning a hard question that you don't know the answer to, but one that challenges your story.

If your first question reads "You say that pizza delivery drivers have the fifth most dangerous job, come on, they're just delivering pizzas, is it really that dangerous?"

That's a challenging question. It's challenging what you're saying, and, it's a great way to lead into your story.

Your last question should always be how the audience can get in contact with you. This is where you will be able to leave your phone number, website, or however you want your customers to be able to get in a hold of you.

At near the end of the question and answer sheet, you will also want to put down a suggested introduction. While newspaper reporters probably won't use this, it's great for a radio host to have to introduce you before the interview.

Here is what our practice question and answer sheet should look like.

Contact Number: (123) 123-1234

Suggested Interview Questions For Paul Baker
Oklahomas Leading Authority On Delivery Driver Safety

1. You say that pizza delivery drivers have the fifth most dangerous job in the United States, come on, they're just delivering pizzas, is it really that dangerous?

2. Why will some pizza restaurants not deliver to certain neighborhoods?

3. So some pizza delivery drivers might not bring the pizza to my front door if I don't have my lights on and my grass hasn't been mowed? Isn't that just the driver not wanting to do their job properly?

4. I've tried to be polite to the driver when they deliver pizza and invite them inside my house, but they always refuse to come in, why is that?

5. You say that you've done over 1000 deliveries yourself over the past nine years, have you ever had any close calls or scary situations?

6. Why are pizza delivery drivers tipped so much less than other businesses that have tipped employees?

7. Is it difficult to keep drivers staffed with the job being as dangerous as it is and with driver tips being small most of the time?

8. How can pizza delivery drivers keep themselves safe and minimize the risk of becoming a target for thieves while performing their job?

9. How can people get in contact with you for more information?

Suggested Introduction for Paul Baker

Paul Baker is a widely recognized as a leading expert and advocate for pizza delivery driver safety. Over the past nine years he has had over 300 delivery drivers work for him, and has personally delivered over 1000 pizza delivery orders himself.

# # #

Notice again how we finish the page with the three pound symbols. Now that we have our question and answer sheet done, let's jump to the next section and see how we put this all together.

Getting Your Press Release Out

So now you have your press release, your biography sheet, and your question and answer sheet finished, so now you're probably wondering what to do with each of them.

Now we need to get these into the hands of the media and start getting some publicity from them. How are we going to do this? We are going to fax your press release to them. Hang on to your other two sheets, we'll need those later.

Notice I said fax, not email or snail mail, but fax. I know a lot of people think that the fax is dead, and no one uses it anymore, but faxing is what you must do if you want to get your press release into the hands of a reporter.

I realize that everyone emails everything in this day and age, but it's just to risky to email your press release to a reporter. They get literally hundreds, if not thousands of emails every day, and simply don't have the time to go through each one of them.

And there's also the problem with the email actually getting into their inbox in the first place. If you email out your press release to several media outlets at one time, it might get labeled as spam.

And some media outlets have trash email accounts that never even get opened or looked at. It's just an account for people to email to, thinking their actually having a shot at contacting someone in that company.

You're much safer faxing it, and if less people are faxing nowadays, that will make your press release more likely to be seen coming from a fax machine than from email.

The only exception to this email rule is if the reporter has already contacted you, and asks you to email them something. In this case, it's ok to send an email. You will just want to ask the reporter what you should put into the subject line so the reporter will know it's from you and not accidentally skip over, or delete it.

If this is your first shot at trying to get publicity, I would suggest faxing your press release out to about 20-30 small newspapers with a circulation of around 1000. If you want to fax it out to radio stations, fax it out to small stations that only have a few hundred watts.

It won't take you very many interviews to get some experience where you can start going to bigger newspapers and radio stations.

You may be tempted, but don't do this! When you first start out, the temptation may be there to fax your press release out to several thousand media outlets in the attempt to get more publicity. Don't do this at first!

If by some stroke of luck, your story takes off and you have several hundred media outlets calling you at one time to get your story, you going to be in trouble.

And, without some experience under your belt, you're not going to be able to give the best interview you're capable of. And if you give a bad interview, it makes it very difficult to get any more interviews later on.

Like almost everything else, it takes practice and experience to get good at doing interviews.

It would be like if you wanted to learn to fly a plane. You go and sit in the class for a few days and learn the basics of flight, then the instructor takes you out and gives you an F-16 fighter jet to fly your first time out.

You probably wouldn't even get off the runway without killing yourself. Same thing with publicity. If your first interview is on the Howard Stern show, you're probably not going to give a very good interview and kill your chances of doing any more interviews in the future.

Start small, learn the ropes, and get some experience under your belt. Plus, by doing these smaller interviews first, you can start adding those to your biography sheet.

Here's another rule to follow when playing the publicity game. Never, under any circumstances call the reporter to see if they received your fax.

I'm going to repeat that because it's so important. Never, under any circumstances call the reporter to see if they received your fax. They don't want to hear from you. When you call them to check on your press release, you're telling them you don't know how to play the game.

Think how you feel on a Friday night. You're really busy, tickets keep piling up, you're staff is just barely keeping up with the orders and then you get a phone call right in the middle of all this near chaos. You answer the phone and what do you hear? "Hi this is Ben, I turned in an application today and wanted to see if you've looked over it yet."

Sorry Ben, you just shot yourself in the ass. Same situation with the reporter, they have time constraints and deadlines to meet. They don't have time to answer every phone call and tell you whether or not they received your press release and have had a chance to look over it or not.

So back to faxing your press release.

When starting out, just use your own fax machine. Unless your fax machine is ancient, you should be able to put in up to 100 fax numbers and then have the machine fax to them all.

You will most likely in the beginning of your quest for publicity never fax out more than 100 faxes at a time. After you have done some interviews, and know what kind of response you'll get from your press release, you might want to consider using a fax broadcasting service.

These fax broadcasting services can crank out over 600 faxes every two minutes, so if you have several thousand faxes to send out, this would be the way to go. The rates to use a fax broadcasting service can range from 6 cents a page, all the way up to 27 cents per page, so make sure to shop around before committing to one.

You might be thinking "why would I want to fax out over 1000 faxes to media outlets that are not in my hometown?" There is a big advantage to doing this, and we'll cover that in a later section of this course.

Remember, when faxing out your press release, you want to fax your press release only and not your biography sheet and questions and answer sheet.

Faxing all three sheets will let the reporter know you don't know how to play the game, so all we're going to fax out initially is the press release.

Never put a cover page on your press release either. Just fax the one page just like it is.

So now we have our press release faxed out. Let's jump to the next section to see what we should do when the reporter calls.

When The Reporter Calls

Ok, so we have our press release faxed out, and reporters are beginning to call you to inquire about your story.

Now when the reporter calls you, they're not really inquiring about your story. Nope, their giving you a test. A test to see if you know how to play the game.

They're going to ask a few questions when they call you, and how you answer these questions are very critical to you getting the interview.

Here's how the first question will go.

Reporter: "Hi, Paul Baker please"

You: "This is Paul"

Reporter: "Hi Paul, this is John Sanders with KMRD radio in Los Angeles. I got your fax. Tell me some more about your story"

<u>This is your first test to see if you know how to play the game.</u> The reporter doesn't really want to know more about your story. They just want to know two things about you.

First, is if you're a nut job, and the second is if you can get to the point in less than 30 seconds.

So if you start telling the reporter… "Well, I got into the pizza business because I saw an angel in a dream, and the angel told me to sell pizzas to save the world from….

Yep, you're a nut job. The reporter will probably tell you something like "Wow, that sounds like an interesting story, can I call you next week to set up an interview"

If the reporter tells you this, then you probably blew it. 99.9% of the time, the reporter, if interested in the story will set up the interview time right then and there, or ask if you have time to do one right now.

By telling you that they'll call you back, they are just getting you off the phone, they will never call back.

Getting to the point of your story is just as important as not being a nut job. They want you to tell them about your story, because they want to see if you can get to the point. The reporter doesn't have time for you to go on and on about your story, especially if you're doing a radio interview.

They want to know that you can get right to the point, and quickly. So if they ask about your story, and you take five minutes to explain it to them, you've probably blown it.

Remember when we worked on our press release, how we got to the point of our story in three sentences or less? This is what you need to do with the reporter.

You don't have to necessarily keep it as brief as your press release was, but you do need to get right to the point and not beat around the bush.

Ok, so we've passed the first part of the reporters test. You've proven to the reporter that you can get right to the point, and you've shown them that you're not a nut job.

Now comes the next part of the test.

The reporter will ask you if you have any additional material you can send him. <u>The only answer the reporter wants to hear from you is "I have a biography sheet and a question and answer sheet I can fax over to you as soon as we finish this phone call</u>.

That's the only answer the reporter is looking for. So many people completely screw this part of the test up by saying two words that lets the reporter know their dealing with someone who doesn't know the rules. Those two words are… "Like what?"

When the reporter asks if you have anything else you can send them, and your answer is "like what", or "such as" you've just shown the reporter you don't know the game.

If you do answer "like what," the reporter probably will tell you what they need, and you can tell them that you can put something together for them, but at that point, you've already blown it.

If the reporter happens to not ask for any other materials, you should tell the reporter that you have a biography sheet and a question and answer sheet available if it would help them out. They will love you for offering it, because you've just made their job a whole lot easier.

Now there's one more hurdle you need to get over before you finish you phone conversation with the reporter.

When the reporter suggests the two of you set up an interview, you immediately need to ask the reporter...

"Will there be any problem with me giving out my contact information?"

What you've just asked the reporter is if he's going to do his job and sell your product.

Some of them might ask you "what do you mean by give out your contact information?" You'll tell the reporter that you want to give out the phone number to your store, or if you have a new website up, you may want to give that.

Most reporters will have no problem at all with this, however, a few will give you the "it's against company policy" line of crap. This is usually the reporter just not knowing their company rules and playing it on the safe side.

At this point, you have one of two options, you can do the interview with no contact information, or you can tell the reporter that you won't be able to do the interview.

You can try to convince the reporter to allow you to give out your contact information by saying something like "I'm sorry, but I don't think I will be able to do the interview with you. I'm giving you a great story to run, and a lot of good information. What's in it for me?"

This will usually get most of the reporters to see that their working with someone who knows how to play the game, and they'll give in and let you give out your contact information

There is that small number of reporters though, that will just absolutely refuse to budge on the contact information issue, and at this point you need to make the decision of whether or not it would be worth your time to do the interview.

Usually if you run into a problem with a reporter with giving out your contact information, it will usually be with someone in the newspaper media.

Radio guys know the rules, and will plug almost anything you want to sell if you give them a great interview and make them look good for their audience.

If you did a great interview, and were selling frozen turds on a stick, the radio host would probably tell his audience how great your frozen turds on a stick are, and how everyone needs to get one.

Back to setting up the interview.

You always want to have an appointment book of some kind handy when the reporter calls so you can write down the date and time of the interview. You do this so you don't accidentally double book yourself.

If you're getting to the point that you're sending out several hundred press releases at one time, and start getting numerous bookings, you're not going to be able to remember the dates and times of all the interviews or follow ups.

You also need to make sure that you write down when, and to who, you send your biography sheet and question sheet too, this way you don't forget to send them, or accidentally send them twice to the same reporter.

If you and the reporter are in different time zones, <u>verify with the reporter which time zone you are using to set up your interview</u>.

It's not uncommon for the reporter to have so much going on, that he might tell you "let's book an interview for Tuesday, June 3rd at 4 PM.

Is that 4 PM his time, or your time? Because if he's on the east coast, and you're on the west coast, he might be trying to call you at 1 PM your time, when it's 4 PM his time.

You might be slaving away in your store finishing up the lunch rush at that time, or you might have another interview set up at 1 PM your time. Always verify the time zone so there's no confusion.

Always verify the number that the reporter needs to call you back at for the interview, and ask the reporter for a direct contact number so incase a problem comes up, you can reach them and let them know.

Now let's jump to the next section and see what happens during the interview.

The Interview

So you've passed all the questions the reporter has thrown at you to see if you know how to play the publicity game. You have your interview date set, and now, if this is one of your first few interviews, you're probably starting to get a little bit nervous.

Before you get too nervous, there's some good news. Almost all of your interviews will be on the phone, and will feel like you're talking to only one person! If you're talking to a newspaper reporter, the only person listening to you is the reporter.

There's really no pressure whatsoever. The reporter might have you repeat something to clarify what you say, but there's no real pressure on you. You're basically just giving one person some information, and they're writing it down.

Radio interviews might seem a little more daunting at first because you might think that there will be a lot of people listening. But once you get on the phone with the host, it's only going to feel like you and the host are having a conversation between two people.

Ever listen to those big talk shows like Rush Limbaugh or Howard Stern? Do the people that call in ever sound nervous? Nope. Do their guests ever sound nervous? Nope again. Why do you think that is? Because when you are talking to the host, it just feels like you're talking to one person on the phone.

There might be several million people listening to your conversation, but it won't feel that way. One of the best things to do is to start off small like we talked about in a previous section.

There are some radio stations so small that they are lucky if they can transmit 150 yards, God knows how these stations stay in business, but find some stations that only have about 50 to100 watts and do a few interviews with them until you get comfortable doing radio interviews.

If you should happen to really screw up, nobody is going to hear it.

Because you're doing these interviews from home and on your phone, you can do whatever you need to get comfortable. Do the interview in bed, have a beer sitting beside you, heck, do the interview naked if you want, nobody is going to know!

When doing your interviews, try to use a land line if possible. With todays technology, cell phones are a lot more dependable than they used to be, but just in case, if possible, use the land line.

When the radio host or reporter starts the interview, and their first question is the first question you put on your question and answer sheet, you know that more likely than not, the reporter will go right down your list of questions and make it an easy interview for you.

When the reporter is finished with the interview, they will probably ask you if it's ok to contact you again if they have any further questions. The answer to this question is a definite yes, and you also want to let the reporter know that they can contact you anytime they have any questions about the subject your interviewing on.

One more quick thing to talk about before we jump to the next section. Some people have the idea that reporters are out to make people look bad by reporting their stories or subjects in a negative way.

This rarely ever happens. I'm not sure if people just watch too much television and see reporters portrayed as mean spirited people whose only ambition is to make someone look bad in front of thousands of people.

Fact is, most reporters are super nice people that are just trying to do their job. You don't have to worry about them writing up a bad story about you, unless you're doing something bad or illegal.

If you're having a big sale for charity, and are then pocketing the cash and not donating what you said you were going to give, then the reporter has an obligation to question you on your actions and print what you're really doing.

But would this really be the reporters fault or yours?

As long as you're being honest, you have nothing to worry about.

So now you know how to write a press release, a biography sheet and a question and answer sheet.

You now know why it's so important to have all three of these sheets, and not just a press release as most people do.

You now know how a reporter will test you when they call to see if you know how to play the game.

But what you might be wondering right now, is why there would be any benefit to doing interviews outside your stores town or neighborhood.

Here's the simple answer. The more interviews you do with newspapers, radio stations and television stations, the more of a celebrity you become, and people like to do business with celebrities.

When people come into your store and you have dozens of newspaper articles hanging from the walls, that's powerful. When they call your store, and have to be put on hold, and hear a radio interview with you, that's powerful. When a customer is eating or waiting or their order, and there's a television showing the interviews you've done on TV, that's powerful.

If someone should ask you why they should do business with you, instead of rattling off some self serving slogan, show them a stack of newspaper articles of interviews you did, and tell them that USA Today can probably do a better job telling them why they should buy from you than from one of your competitors.

Publicity is powerful, plain and simple. The more you get, the more your sales will skyrocket.

So now that you know how to get publicity, go out and get it, there's no reason for you not to, after all… it's free!

Publicity Media Resources

The following is a list of resource directories you can use to find and contact different newspaper, radio, and television media to fax you press releases to. Some of these are very expensive to purchase (Bacons will set you back over $700) and there are some that are very inexpensive.

The more expensive ones usually have a more thorough listing, so my first recommendation would be to check your local library for a copy of them before spending that much money. Some of them, like Dustbooks provides a directory of only the small media outlets and sells for less than $39 bucks. This directory would be an excellent first choice for someone just starting out with publicity and trying to get some experience.

If you are just going to stick to your own local market for publicity, a simple google search will bring up the available media contacts and their contact info.

Dustbooks
P.O. Box 100, Paradise, CA 95967
530-877-6110
www.dustbooks.com

Oxbridge Communications Inc.
186 5th Ave., New York, NY 10010
800-955-0231
www.mediafinder.com

Bacons Media Directory
332 S. Michigan Ave. Suite 900, Chicago, IL 60604
866-639-5087
www.cision.com

Gebbies
P.O. Box 1000, New Paltz, NY 12561
845-255-7560
www.gebbieinc.com

BurrellesLuce
75 East Northfield Road Livingston, NJ 07039
800-368-8070
www.burrellesluce.com

Gale Research
27500 Drake Road, Farmington Hill, MI 48333
800-877-4253
www.gale.com

The $500 Launch

If you're in a financial position where you have severely limited funds and need to get the biggest bang for your buck as quickly as possible, then this section will give you a road map to slowly building your sales with a small $500 budget.

If you're fortunate enough to have the capital to make a larger investment, then by all means, go right for your competitors jugular and roll out a direct mail letter campaign, dropping 1000-2000 letters per week.

However, if you can't afford to let go of a couple grand right away, then this is a safe, low investment route to take.

Because we have only $500 to work with, we can't waste it on people we are not sure will buy, so we will be focusing on your current customer base to get things rolling.

We know that the people in our customer base eat pizza, and have ordered from us before. This will make our marketing much less risky than spending our money on people that may or may not eat much pizza.

To keep track of what we're spending, and what our potential return might be, we'll assume you're currently running $20,000 per month in sales.

Start by raising prices.

Go through your menu and raise your prices by as much as you can. A five or ten percent increase would be a good start. If the average price of your pizzas is $10, then just by raising prices by 5%, then you're looking at a potential sales increase of $1000 per month.

Because there's no cost to raise prices, this is pure profit.

2000 pizzas per month x .50 price increase (5%) = $1000

The next strategy we'll use is the "Thank You" bounce back card.

We're going to pass out 20 of these cards per day, so you will need 12 50ct boxes of these to get you through the next 30 days. Our cost for the 12 boxes will be $70.44 ($5.87 x 12).

I had an average return rate on this strategy of 63%, but to play it on the safe side, we'll cut that by more than half and plan on a response rate of only 30%. So within 30 days after handing out your last card, you should have close to 180 of these redeemed.

If each person orders one large pizza, and gets an order of breadsticks for free, we should still be able to keep our food cost at under 35%. So we have $10.50 per order minus $3.68 food cost giving us a net profit of $6.82 per order.

$6.82 per order x 180 = $1227.60

$1227.60 - $70.44 for cost of cards = $1157.60 net profit

Next we'll implement the "Lazy Customer" strategy. Sending letter to our customers who haven't ordered in the past 30 days. My average was 350 letters every month to lazy customers that had hit the 30 day mark.

My profit after offering the free calizone averaged $7.74 per order, and I had an average response rate of over 21% using letters.

350 letters x .50 each = $175.00
73 letters redeemed (21%) x 7.74 profit = $565.02
$565.02 - $175.00 = 390.02 net profit

Once we have our lazy customer letters ready to go, we'll set up our voice broadcasting. This will cost us $126.95 to set up.

Normally you would mail out your lazy customer letters on a daily basis. However, this time, we're going to mail one weeks worth of letters out on Thursday, so they hit the mailbox on Friday.

We also wouldn't usually use the voice broadcasting on the lazy customer letters, however we will for our initial launch to get the most response that we can.

When you have one weeks worth of lazy customer letters ready to mail, call your voice broadcasting center and record the message just like it is in the section on voice broadcasting. By doing this, we will be able to increase our response rate on our lazy customer letters by up to an additional 30%.

So now instead of getting a 21% response, we're now looking at getting around a 50% response on our mailing.

350 letters x .50 each = $175.00
175 letters redeemed (50%) x 7.74 profit = $1354.50
$1354.50 – 175.00 - $126.95 = $1052.05 net profit

The final tactic we'll include in our $500 launch will be the everyone wins contest.

During the first 30 days while your passing out your thank you cards, and mailing out your lazy customer letters, be handing out the contest cards and have the drawing held no more than 6 weeks after you start passing out the cards.

The initial cost of your cards will be $65.00. Keeping our total initial launch cost at $437.39, under the $500 budget we set up.

At the end of the promotion, after the drawing for the grand prize, you should have more than enough profit from the other tactics to cover the cost of mailing out the 500 letters to all the people who entered and didn't win.

If our numbers hold the same as our results in the section on the "Everyone wins contest" our profit should be close to $2,410.00.

So within 60 days of starting this campaign, our total return on our investment of $437.39 should be…

Prices raised - $1000
Thank you cards - $1157.60
Lazy customer letters with voice broadcasting -
$1052.05
Everyone wins contest - $2,410.00

Total Net Profit = <u>$5619.65</u>

Your profits could be higher or lower than this depending on how many cards you pass out and how many lazy customers you send letters to.

However, even if your profits were only half of the $5619.65, that's more than enough to snowball your funds into a direct mail letter campaign, which is where the monster profits are.

What To Do When
<u>A Competitor Shuts Down</u>

This is one of my favorite techniques to quickly add customers and cash to your business. The trick to maximizing this techniques effectiveness is to pay close attention to your local competition.

If you've been in business for any amount of time, you eventually see one of your competitors shut down and go out of business. This can be for a variety of reasons, but usually and most often, it involves finances.

Most get to the point that their not making enough money, or maybe they borrowed so much money when they opened, that after a few years they can't afford to make the payments anymore.

In any case, when you see a competitor shut down, you <u>immediately</u> need to do two things.

First. Immediately call the telephone company and see if you can get their old phone number. Either have the number forwarded to your store, or physically installed in your store. Usually when a competitor closes they have their phone lines shut off to avoid collections from creditors.

Second. If there's a certain number of days you have to wait to acquire a phone number, or if your competitor hasn't shut it off, you can approach your competitor and offer to purchase his old number for cash.

The amount will vary depending on the business and how many customers he had, but chances are, if your competitors broke, he'll be interested in trading something he can't use anymore for some quick cash.

By doing this, you're taking advantage of any advertising that your competitor has recently done, and will now have all of their customers going straight to your business instead of to another one of your competitors.

And when one of their old customers calls and gets you instead, you just need to explain that you're now taking care of so-and-so's customers. You might even give them some kind of discount or freebie just because they used to be so-and-so's former customer.

So how profitable is this tactic?

This is how the numbers worked out for me when I used this strategy on a mom and pop pizza store that had shut down.

I ended up paying the owners of the store $500 bucks to have their old number forwarded to my store. I never got to see their actual customer list (if they even kept one) but judging from the number of phone calls, I was guessing that they had around 500-700 regular customers.

We offered everyone that we knew was a previous customer of the other store half off on their first order. By the end of three months, we had over 600 new customers in our data base.

We had over 300 of those customers order a second time, and 86 of those customers became regular customers, ordering at least once a month, sometimes twice a month for the next year.

So here's the numbers.

Our average order per customer at the time was $16.00, and we gave them half off. That's $8.00 per order, and after you subtract the food cost for us to make the pizza of about $3.00 per pizza, that gives us a net profit of about $5.00 per customer.

600 new customers x $5.00 = $3000

That was over a 3 month period. Not a bad return over three months on a $500 dollar investment. But wait…

About half of those original 600 people ordered a second time at full price, which then gave me about $13.00 in profit for each customer.

300 repeat customers x $13.00 = $3,900

And like I said, 86 of those customers became regular customers. My regular customers had an average order of about $18.00 per order. They would usually add on 2liters or breadsticks, making their average order a little bit higher. Usually I could count on my regular customers bringing me in about $336 each in profit every year.

86 regular customers x $336 each = $28,896 yearly

Just by adding those 86 regular customers, I increased my yearly bottom line profit by $28,896! And that's on a $500 investment!

The number of customers your competitors have will probably vary greatly depending on how they ran their business. Some stores my only have a few customers, and some may have thousands.

You need to decide how much each customer is worth so you don't overpay for any new customers you will acquire by using this strategy. Most competitors that you approach however, won't view the transaction as you buying their customers, they'll see it as you buying their existing phone line, and this is very good for you.

Someones phone line really isn't worth much, however, the customers that will call that phone line, and get your store, are worth thousands!

If you don't use the strategy, you're letting tons of new customers and cash disperse to your other competitors instead of having them funneled to yours.

This is another reason for keeping an accurate customer list. The money is always in the list. No matter what type of business I'm looking at purchasing, I always want to see the customer list.

If the business doesn't have a list, (which most don't) the business isn't worth nearly as much as one that has a large, carefully maintained list.

In a worst case scenario, if you're forced to sell your business, having a large active customer list makes your business more valuable, and you could probably get a higher price for your store, or if you're looking at buying out an existing store, always ask to see their list.

A store with 10,000 names on their list is much more valuable than a store with only 1000 names.

<u>255 Of The Greatest Headlines Ever Written</u>

Here's a listing of 255 of the greatest headlines that have ever been written. These headlines have been responsible for countless millions of dollars in sales. While these headlines don't specifically relate to pizza, restaurants or food service, they are excellent templates and inspiration to use when creating your own headlines.

The Secret Of Bowling Strikes

Have You A "Worry" Stock?

They Shocked Us. They Outraged Us. They Didn't Do Anything Wrong – They Just Did it first

What Would You Rather Do This Evening: Watch TV Or Make Some Real Money?

How To Find Someone To Love

Pregnant? The Sooner You Know, The Better.

Can Your Child Read These Words?

Are You Too Busy Earning A Living To Make Any Money?

How To Make Money With Display Ads

How to Write A Business Letter

The Secret Of Making People Like You

Some Straight Talk About Earning Extra Income

How Often Do You Hear Yourself Saying: "No I Haven't Read It; I've Been Meaning Too!"

"Insider Information" – On Who's Really Making Money – Plus Exactly How Those Businesses Operate.

Watch Your Weight And Inches Disappear

161 New Ways To A Man's Heart – In This Fascinating Book For Cooks.

The Deaf Now Hear Whispers

Again She Orders ... "A Chicken Salad, Please"
The Child Who Won The Hears Of All

Reduce Office Turnover By 100%

If You Read Music You'll Love Our Magazine

Have You Ever Taken A Practice Golf Swing At A Dandelion?

Are You Ever Tongue-Tied At A Party?

7 Ways To Collect Your Unpaid Bills

This Is Marie Antoinette – Riding To Her Death

The Last 2 Hours Are The Longest – And Those Are The 2 Hours Save

No Office – No Phones – No Hassles – Just Cold Hard Cash In The Mail!

Thousands Have This Priceless Gift – But Never Disclose It!

Hands That Look Lovelier In 24 Hours – Or Your Money Back

How To Start From "Scratch" And Become a P.O. Box Millionaire

The Most Expensive Mistake Of Your Life

Lost For Words? Push The Buttons And Voila!

**For The Woman Who Is Older Than She Looks
How To Develop A Silver Tongue, A Golden Touch And A Mind Like A Steel Trap**

Have You Ever Seen A Grown Man Cry?

Where You Can Go In A Good Used Car

Test Your Ability To Ever Grow Up

Life In The Fast Lane

67 Reasons Shy It Would Have Paid You To Answer Our Ad A Few Months Ago

Mobile Money Maker

Need More Money?

Suppose This Happened On Your Wedding Day!

How To Do Wonders With A Little Land

One Transaction Can Make You Independent For The Rest Of Your Life

Imagine Working Until 4:00 A.M. – And Loving Every Minute Of It!

New Rubber Stamp Business Pays Beginners Up To $16.50 An Hour!

Want To Be A Legal Investigator?

Stop Dreaming And Start Making Money

Don't Let Athlete's Foot "Lay You Up"

To Men Who Want To Quit Work Someday

Make Extra Cash Writing Advertising Book Match Covers

What's Your Best Chance Of Earning $50,000 A Year By The Time You Are 30?

Tom McCahill Says: "The Appliance Repair Field Is So Uncrowded It's Almost Lonely"

My Feet Were Killing Me... Until I Discovered The Miracle In Germany

Too Busy Earning A Living To Make Any Money?

"Last Friday... Was I Scared! – My Boss Almost Fired Me!"

Fatten Your Bank Account

Why These Vitamins Can Make You Feel Peppier

What Everybody Ought To Know... About This Stock And Bond Business

Today... Add $10,000 To Your Estate – For The Price Of A New Hat

"No Time For Yale – Took College At Home", Says Well Known Author

It's Easy To Cash In On Your Amazing Astrological Abilities

Are They Being Promoted Right Over Your Head?

How To Plan Your House To Suit Yourself Are We A Nation Of Low-Brows?

Would You Like To Take In $140 After Supper?

Inventors, Strike Pay Dirt!

Throw Away Your Oars!

We're Looking For People To Write Children's Books

How To Pay Less For Advertising While You Get More Orders

Greatest Gold Mine Of Easy "Things-To-Make" Ever Crammed Into One Big gook

How To Give Your Children Extra Iron – These 3 Delicious Ways

Don't Envy The Plumber – Be One

Don't Try This With Any Other Copier

Free Book – Tells You 12 Secrets Of Better Lawn Care

Whose Fault When Children Disobey?

Call Back These Great Moments At The Opera

Right And Wrong Farming Methods – And Little Pointers That Will Increase Your Profits

New Pill Gives Almost Complete Relief From Arthritis Pain!

The Amazing Secret Of A Marketing Genius Who Is Afraid To Fly

Speak Spanish Like A Diplomat

"Some Straight Talk About Vitamins And Your Sex Life"

This Almost Magical Lamp Lights Highway Turns Before you Make Them

New Shampoo Leaves Your Hair Smoother – Easier To Manage

How To Overcome The Body Chemical That Keeps You Fat!

It's A Shame For You Not To Make Good Money – When These Men Do It So Easily

Announcing… The New Edition Of The Encyclopedia That Makes It Fun To Learn Things
You Can Only Go So Far On BS

Can You Pass This Memory Test?

Who Else Wants Lighter Cake – In Half The Mixing Time?

Buy No Desk… Until You've Seen This Sensation Of The Business Show

Desperate Woman Loses 277 Pounds With Amazing New Diet Secret!

Ohio Man Discovers The Secret Of How To Escape The American Rat Race

New Cake – Improver Gets You Compliments Galore!

How To Write A Good Advertisement

California Lawyer Discovers How To Make Money At Home With the Help Of The U.S. Government

It's Crazy That A High School Dropout Would Make This Much Money

Did You Ever See A "Telegram" From Your Heart?

Where The Money Is And How To Get It

The Lowdown On Self Publishing

Pierced By 301 Nails… Retains Full Air Pressure

How To Make A Killing In Closeouts

How Much Is "Worker Tension" Costing Your Company?

The Secret Of Teaching Yourself Music

Who Else Wants to Make Big Money In Electronics

New "Energy Pill" Tested By U.S. Marines With Amazing Results

The Amazing Diet Secret Of A Frustrated Cleburne Housewife

An Open Letter To Every Overweight Person In Portland

How To Burn Off body Fat, Hour-By-Hour!

How The Experts Buy And Sell Gold And Silver

You Can't Become Rich In Your Pocket Until You Become Rich In Your Mind!

Famed Physicist Proves That Sitting In A Pyramid Causes Unexplainable Good Thing To Happen

How To Beat The Bank At Their Own Game

How To Discover The Fortune That Lies Hidden In Your Head

Do You Make These Mistakes In English?

Do You Sincerely Want To Be Rich?

Scientists Discover Mystery Chemical That Seems To Drive Women Wild!

Here's How To Find Out If Your Bank Is About To Go Bankrupt!

Want To Be An Airline Flight Attendant?

Which Of These 5 Skin Trouble Would You Like To End?

They Laughed When I Sat Down To At The Piano – But When I Started To Play!

Former Barber Earns $8,000 In 4 Months As A Real Estate Specialist

Does Uncle Sam Owe You Money You Don't Even Know About?

You Don't Have To Die To Collect On Your Insurance Policy

How Your Horoscope Can Bring You Wealth, Love, Success And Happiness

Why People In Vermont Are Healthier, Less Overweight, Stay Young Longer, Live Longer Than People Of Any Other State In The Union

The Amazing Secrets Of The Hottest Investment Of the Last 5 Years!

Why Some Foods "Explode" In Your Stomach

Lawyer Reveals Legal Loopholes That Make Money

Now! Own Florida Land this Easy Way… $10 Down and $10 A Month

Fountain Of Youth Discovered By Little Know Civilization Over 2300 Years Ago

The Crimes We Commit Against Our Stomachs

How To Write Copy That Will Make You Rich

To People Who Want To Write – But Can't Get Started

The Machine That Peels Off Pounds While You Sit Back And Enjoy It

New Diet Burns Off More Fat Than If You Ran 98 Miles A Week!

The Amazing $10.00 Fake Diamond That Will Fool 9 Out Of 10 Jewelers

What's Your Best Chance To Make Money In Real Estate Today? The Answer Below May Surprise You.

How To Improve Your Memory

The Man With The "Grasshopper Mind"

How To Wake Up The Financial Genius Inside You

The Chinese Secrets Of Weight Control
Full Time Minister Finds Part Time Goldmine!

The Amazing Lost Money Secret Of The U.S.
Government

Want To Lose Some Weight?

Alive With Pleasure

New Pill for Diet Failures Lets You Burn Off Body Fat
24 Hours A Day!

By This Time Next Month, You Could Have A Global
Data Communications Network

How To Get Rich Reading Classified Ads

Corporation Uses Magazine Articles As Marketing Key

The Amazing Beverly Hills "Wrinkle Eraser"
Discovered By A Top Oriental Chemist!

Are You An Educated Underachiever?
Costa Mesa Man Swears Under Oath That His New
"Energy Pill" Does Not Contain Cocaine Or Any Other
Illegal Stimulant – "It's A Food, Not A Drug"

To The Traveling Salesman Who's Smart Enough To
Know When To Call It Quits

The "10 Quickest Ways" To Get More Customers

Do You Have These Symptoms Of Nervous Exhaustion?

How To Form Your Corporation Without A Lawyer For Under $50.00

"You Kill That Story – Or I'll Run You Out Of The State!"

Important News For Folks Who Swore They Would Never Try Another Reducing Product

The Most Expensive Magazine In The World. Yet Over 40,000 Businessmen Buy It Every Month. Why?

A Breakthrough Idea For Those Who Want To Act In The Movies

How To Get A Free Supply Of An Amazing New Diet Pill That Works Like Crazy!

How To Get Out Of The Rat Race And Into The Chips

Check The Kind Of Body You Want

How You Can Make Money With The Arabs

Here's A Quick Way To Break Up A Cold

He Became Twice The Man At Half The Weight!

You Never Saw Such Letters As Harry And I Got About Our Pears

How A "Fool Stunt" Made Me A Star Salesman

Chicago Man Reveals A Shortcut To Authorship

An Amazing Business You Can Carry In Your Pocket

7 Ways Long Distance Can Keep Your Head Above Water

How To Pay Zero Taxes!

An Educated Failure
When Doctors "Feel Rotten" This Is What They Do

Doctor Discovers Method Of Regaining Hair Loss

The Other Side Of The Story On Rock Hudson

How Much Are You Losing To Deadbeats Right Now?

But What If You Could See Her Naked?
Free Kit Tells How To Take Better Photographs

Here's A Way To Make Money That Has Never Yet Failed

Moneymaking Sledgehammer

The Secret Of Having Good Luck

The Secret Of Perfect Putting

Tested Advertising Methods

"...The Amazing thing, Of Course, Is The Speed At Which This Program Works. It Is Rather Remarkable To Throw Off As Much As 6 Pounds Of Fluid And Fat In The Very First Weekend..."

Think And Grow Rich

How A New Discovery Made A Plain Girl Beautiful

Who Else Wants A Screen Star Figure

The Ugly Truth About Your New Car

If You Read Nothing Else – Read This

Who's Making A Bundle?

How Bad A Beating Are You Willing To Take To Own A New Car?

Why Some People Almost Always Make Money In The Stock Market

How You Can Legally Profit From "Insider" Information On The Stock Market

The Amazing Diet Secret Of A Desperate Housewife

Image Being Such A Great Lover Women Can See It In Your Eyes!

Science Has Finally Counterfeited A Perfect Diamond
How To Make Money Writing Short Paragraphs

Doctors Discover The Cellulite Dissolver

Confessions Of A Disbarred Lawyer

"I Had Been Overweight For 10 Years, So… My Friends Could Hardly Believe Their Eyes When They Saw Me Lose 56 Pounds In Only 6 Weeks!"

What's Wrong With This Picture?

**There's Another Woman Waiting For Every Man –
And She's Too Smart To Have "Morning Mouth"**

**Man Who Limped With Foot Pain – Now Runs 2 Miles
Every Day!**

**If You Can Read This And Write Simple English, I'll
Show You How To Make Money Selling Words**

**"Send Me To Any City In The United States. Take
Away My Wallet. Give Me $100.00 For Living
Expenses And In 72 Hours I'll Buy You An Excellent
Piece Of Real Estate Using <u>None</u> Of My Own Money."**

**My Name Is Paul Franklin… And I'd Like To Make A
Confession!**

How To Raise And Train Your Puppy

**Imagine Me… Holding An Audience Spellbound For 30
Minutes!**

Are You Tired Of The Treatment Your Getting?

**You Don't Know Me, I Realize… But I Want You To
Have This Before It's Too Late**

How To Push Your Resume To The Top Of The Stack

How To Win Friends And Influence People

**The 5 Most Costly Mistakes In Business – How Many
Are You Making Right Now?**

Does Your Child Ever Embarrass you?

The Secret Of Making People Like You

Have You Ever Bowled A Strike And Said, "I've Got It!"?

How To Get $373,500 Out Of A $300,000 House

How To Get What The U.S. Government Owes YOU!

The Secret Of How America's Number One Handicapper "Stole" Over $1,000,000 From The Racetracks Last Year

How To Discover The Priceless Secret Of Good Health And Slash Your Medical Bills In Half!

New! Your Child Is The Star Of This Brand New Sesame Street Storybook!

Here Are 133 Surprise Ways To Get Money From Washington D.C.

Get Out Of Debt in 90 Minutes Without Borrowing!

Released At Last – 137 Perfectly Legal Ways To Get A Check Out Of Uncle Sam!

The Inside Story Of A Business That Requires So Little Of Anything, You Could Run It Out Of A Phone Booth

The Amazing Blackjack Secret Of A Las Vegas Mystery Man!

Have You Ever Said, "I Just Can't Seem To Concentrate"?

New Help For Not So Perfect Hair

17 Stocks You Should Dump Right Away

He Was 24 Pounds Of Sweet Tooth

Little Leaks That Keep Men Poor

7 Steps To Freedom

The $12,000 Housewife

How I Made A Fortune With A "Fool Idea"

**At 5 For 99 Cents, You Can Indulge Your Fantasies
This Month**

**Often A Bridesmaid, Never A Bride
Guaranteed To Go Thru Ice, Mud Or Snow – Or We
Pay The Tow!**

**How To Obtain Guaranteed Credit Anywhere In The
United States**

World Poker Champ Sells Secrets For $9.95

Banking Secrets That Banks Don't Want Published

Thousands Now Play Who Never Thought They Could

**Movie Actor Reveals Amazing New Weight Loss
Breakthrough**

How To Get 12 Hours Out Of An 8 Hour Day

The Lazy Mans Way To Riches

The Secret Of Sticking To Your Diet

At Last, Someone Has Unlocked The Secret Of Getting People To Fall In Love With You!

How To Flatten Your Tush

Dare To Be Rich

How To Rob Race Tracks Legally

Advice To Wives Whose Husbands Don't Save Money – By A Wife

The Truth About Getting Rich

Profits That Lie Hidden In Your Farm

Reduce While You Sleep

Conclusion To Black Ops Pizza Marketing

In conclusion to Black Ops Pizza Marketing, I'd like to leave you with a story that I was told some years ago that influenced the way I looked at business and marketing.

Imagine a martial artist kneeling before his master sensei in a ceremony to receive a very hard earned black belt.

This martial artist has worked for this belt for over 10 years, relentlessly studying the strikes, kicks, and stances. After all these years, this student has finally reached a pinnacle of achievement in his discipline.

The sensei looks at his student kneeling before him, and says to him "There is yet one more test you must pass before receiving the black belt"

The student looks up at him and says "I am ready sensei," fully expecting to have another round of sparing with multiple opponents, or another demonstration of an extremely difficult kata.

The sensei looks at his student and tells him he must answer this one last essential question… "What is the true meaning of the black belt?"

The student pauses for several minutes, thinking about his answer, then replies. "It is the end of my journey, it is a well deserved reward for all my hard work and dedication."

The sensei looks at his student in silence, clearly not satisfied with his students answer.

"You are not ready for the black belt" the sensei tells the student. "Come back in one year."

One year later, the student is kneeling in front of his sensei again.

"What is the true meaning of the black belt?" asks the sensei.

"It is a symbol of distinction, and the highest level of achievement in our discipline." Answered the student proudly, sure that he had gotten it right this time.

The sensei sat silent for several minutes, clearly not satisfied.

"You are not ready for the black belt" the sensei says. "Come back in one year."

One year later, the student is kneeling once again in front of his sensei.

And again the sensei asks "What is the true meaning of the black belt?"

The student pauses for several seconds, then responds.

"The black belt represents the beginning of a never ending journey of discipline, learning, work, and the pursuit of an ever higher standard."

The sensei waits in silence, lets his students answer sink in, and then says "Yes, you are now ready to receive the black belt, for you now understand that it represents the beginning of your work and not the end."

No matter how good you get at marketing your pizza store, keep discovering and learning new and innovative marketing techniques and adding to your marketing arsenal.

Good luck!

Resources

Letter and menu printing
www.takeoutprinting.com

Postcard and business card printing
www.colorprintingcentral.com

Envelope printing
www.printingyoucantrust.com

Direct mail grabbers
www.lumpymail.com
www.milliondollarbillshop.com
www.millionbill.com
www.3DMailSuccess.com

Voice broadcasting
www.automaticresponse.com
www.automatedmarketingsolutions.com

Free recorded message service
www.itelecenter.com

Mucked up letter software
www.copydoodles.com

Texting service
www.sumotext.com

Warning sticker printing
www.lightninglabels.com

**The author, Paul Baker
is available for individual consulting
schedule permitting.**

**You may contact him by email at
paul@blackopspizzamarketing.com**

www.ingramcontent.com/pod-product-compliance
Lightning Source LLC
Chambersburg PA
CBHW051854170526
45168CB00001B/103